Handbook for Teachers

CW00516846

School Inspection

School Inspection

A teacher's guide to preparing,
surviving & evaluating Ofsted Inspection

Elizabeth Holmes

London: The Stationery Office

Illustration by Nigel Paige.

British Library Cataloguing in Publication Data

A catalogue record for this book is available from the British Library.
ISBN 0 11 702617 4
Printed and bound by The Stationery Office
TJ003180 C20 12/00

Published by The Stationery Office and available from:

The Stationery Office
(mail, telephone and fax orders only)
PO Box 29, Norwich NR3 1GN
General enquiries / Telephone orders 0870 600 5522
Fax orders 0870 600 5533

www.thestationeryoffice.com
www.schoolmanager.net

The Stationery Office Bookshops
123 Kingsway, London WC2B 6PQ
020 7242 6393 Fax 020 7242 6394
68–69 Bull Street, Birmingham B4 6AD
0121 236 9696   Fax 0121 236 9699
33 Wine Street, Bristol BS1 2BQ
0117 926 4306   Fax 0117 929 4515
9–21 Princess Street, Manchester M60 8AS
0161 834 7201   Fax 0161 833 0634
16 Arthur Street, Belfast BT1 4GD
028 9023 8451   Fax 028 9023 5401
The Stationery Office Oriel Bookshop
18-19 High Street, Cardiff CF1 2BZ
029 2039 5548   Fax 029 2038 4347
71 Lothian Road, Edinburgh EH3 9AZ
0870 606 5566   Fax 0870 606 5588

The Stationery Office's Accredited Agents
(see Yellow Pages)

and through good booksellers

Contents

Foreword

The Inspector Calls

Miss, miss, there's a man at the back of the classroom
With a big black book and smile like a crocodile.
Miss, he asked me if I got a lot of homework,
And when I said, 'Too much!' – he wrote it down.

Miss, miss, there's a man at the back of the classroom
With a long sharp pencil and eyes like a shark.
Miss, he asked me what I liked best about our school
And when I said, 'The dinners!' – he wrote it down.

Miss, miss, there's a man at the classroom
With a big square badge and hair like hedgehog.
Miss, I asked him what he *liked about our school,*
and he said he was not there to answer my *questions.*
He said he was just 'a fly on the wall'.

Miss, miss, why don't you tell him to BUZZ OFF!'

(From *Over Hill and Dale* by Gervase Phinn, Michael Joseph)

I should imagine that there are few teachers in the country who would not echo the sentiments in this poem – that the silent and unnerving presence sitting in the corner of the classroom, clipboard on lap, pencil poised, eagle eyes glinting menacingly, would 'buzz off'. There can be little doubt that the word Ofsted fills most teachers with fear and anxiety, causes stress and illness in others and sometimes develops in a deep and abiding dread. And the horror stories about the Ofsted inspector abound:

'She swanned into my classroom without a by-you-leave and left without a word.'

'He stood at the front like a great eastern statue with a face like a death mask.'

'All three of them watched the assembly from the back of the hall like the three monkeys, comparing notes the whole time and not smiling once.'

Recently, on a literature course I was directing, I asked the teachers attending to compose a poem beginning: 'Inspectors expect you to:' It is interesting that not one poem mentioned anything positive about the process of school inspection.

Inspectors expect you to:
plan well,
perform well,
organise well,
manage pupils well,
assess well.
challenge well,
and smile ... as well.

Inspectors expect you to:
teach with care,
have books to share,
plan in detail,
let no-one fail,
be on the ball,

smile at all,
be patient and fair,
and show you care
– every second of every minute of every hour of every day.

Inspectors expect you to:
be planned,
be prepared,
be positive,
be punctual,
And ... be perfect.

Inspectors expect you to:
plan extremely,
prepare endlessly,
teach dramatically,
behave humbly,
react gratefully –
and generally achieve the bloody impossible!

So Ofsted and the inspectors who undertake it get a bad press. Few teachers would welcome an inspection but none would deny that there is a need for an outside and objective assessment on how well their school is doing and in what ways it could improve. What teachers *would* welcome, however, is a practical and clearly written book, free of jargon and gobbledegook, to help them prepare effectively and become fully informed about the process itself. This teacher's guide is just such a text.

School Inspection looks to those facing the dreaded Ofsted. It is not a 'tips for teachers' book but a manual full of sensible advice and really useful information which will hearten teachers and encourage them to prepare for the Ofsted experience in a positive way. The clear structure, interesting examples of good practice, lively commentaries and anecdotes enhance the text and make it very readable and accessible. The pros and cons of inspection and the background to Ofsted are covered, how an inspection team works is described simply, detailed advice is given about the documentary evidence required and how the school's results and pupils' achievements are interpreted and evaluated. The characteristics of an effective teacher and how judgements about him or her are made are considered and there is much, much more to support governors, headteachers and classroom practitioners. What this text does, above all, is to reassure those being evaluated that the inspection process need not be viewed as such a frightening prospect and that school inspectors are not the humourless and insensitive box tickers who have little empathy or understanding of the demanding and challenging role undertaken by the teachers they are observing.

School Inspection is a must for every staffroom bookshelf. It is a valuable resource which will be of real interest and use for those about to grapple with the challenges of Ofsted.

Gervase Phinn
Visiting Professor of Education at Teeside University, formerly Principal Adviser with North Yorkshire County Council and Registered Inspector with HMI.

Acknowledgements

Writing a book such as this cannot be done in isolation. Numerous inspectors, advisors, teachers, headteachers, pupils and parents all contributed ideas and perspectives that helped to shape this book and for this I am extremely grateful. I would also like to thank:

- Charlotte Howard of the Fox and Howard Literary Agency
- Helen Bowen, Wendy Lees, Jane Mayger Brown, Emma Martin and everyone else at The Stationery Office who was involved in this book
- Gervase Phinn, for insights, encouragement and inspiration
- Staff at Ofsted who answered my many enquiries
- Olwyn Gunn of the NASUWT
- Rosa Drohomirecka of the Association of Teachers and Lecturers
- Martin Quaife and Beth Anderson of Worthing High School, Frank Regester of White Styles County Middle School, Andrew Simpson of Boxgrove Church of England Primary School and Geoff Smith of Littlehampton Community School
- Kevin McCarthy of Re:membering Education
- Jason Harding and Sue Furness of the Teacher Support Network
- My family and friends – ever-understanding of deadlines!

E Holmes
July 1999

Introduction

Inspection is an inevitable part of school life. From a child's first day at school to the day that he or she leaves, educational achievement must be accounted for; and those at the front line of this accountability, in the eyes of the ones with a responsibility to provide an educational service, are teachers.

The current system of inspection, managed by the Office for Standards in Education (Ofsted), draws heavily on the National Curriculum and standardised assessment tasks as benchmarks for the standard of the education being offered to the nation's children. This combination of inspection, delivery of the National Curriculum and standardised testing has probably been the most vehemently opposed development in education since the Second World War, attracting the attention (and perhaps igniting the imaginations) of the public and the media.

Yet, of these developments in education, it was the introduction of Ofsted inspections that seems to have caused the teaching profession unprecedented anxiety, and has elicited strong resistance. Even with the passing of time and the benefit of first-hand experience, the anticipation of inspections still holds, for some, the worst of their fears of inadequacy, however adept and skilled they may be at their jobs.

Inspection has been a part of school life since formal education began, and undoubtedly will continue to be central to education policy for the foreseeable future. As far as the Ofsted system of inspection is concerned, this book is not the place to discuss the merits or otherwise of its adopted methods. What the book sets out to do is to highlight the extent of manoeuvrability that teachers have within this system of inspection, and how effective preparation (and correct information) can help to lessen the negative impact that inspection may have. By acknowledging this, inspection can be seen less as an inevitable hurdle in school life, and more as a valuable tool in development.

An often-held view of inspection is that there is an element of 'hoop jumping' involved. This book does not seek to offer tips to this end. What it aims to do is to help teachers maximise the potential for a positive experience of inspection through practical advice and information that can be realistically implemented by those in the classroom.

The advice and information contained in the following chapters draw heavily on the anecdotes, testimonies, ideas and coping mechanisms of those from all corners of educational life. These are individuals with extensive experience of inspection, be it as leaders and managers, teachers or inspectors. In many cases, the advice is time-tested and chosen specifically to encourage teachers to face inspection squarely and with energy, rather than resignation.

There are enormous difficulties in offering a path through the complexities of inspection as we know it today. An inspection forces many teachers outside their comfort zones; zones that are already extraordinarily far-reaching. By laying bare the bones of inspection and all that it can entail, it is hoped that this book will enable you to expand your comfort zone to include, even embrace, regular inspection. That said, significant differences exist between schools and the way in which inspections are anticipated. For this reason, sources of external support have also been indicated where possible.

Research for this book has evoked diverse remarks about inspection from those involved in education. While I write as someone who has experienced many hours of observation in inspection and who, ultimately, enjoyed the opportunities that inspection gave me to focus on my work and receive feedback on it, I have been mindful of the fact that not all teachers feel the same way. For some, inspection holds a cocktail of fear, insecurity, anxiety and apprehension; and for a few, this is thought to have contributed to the most tragic of outcomes.

We are all very different from each other in our perceptions, our strengths and our aptitudes, and so there can be no magic 'fix' to suit all for the professional anxieties we may face. If you would like to contribute your thoughts on how inspection can best be experienced positively, you can e-mail me at: ea.holmes@virgin.net.

While not everything can work for everyone, the ideas in this book will, I hope, help you to thrive rather than survive during your inspection. Better still, they may inspire in you positive and creative responses to whatever inspection has in store.

Checklists and Tables

In order to have the relevant information presented and retrieved with ease, checklists and tables have been used where possible. The intention is not that these lists should be followed without deviation;

rather, they should inspire appropriate solutions to the situations you may face before, during and after an inspection.

'Action' boxes

Sometimes it can be helpful to focus on a potentially problematic aspect of your work in an attempt to draw out solutions. The 'Action' features have been written for this purpose, and do not need to be worked through slavishly.

'Example' boxes

All of the examples are real experiences, although names have been excluded. In order to highlight or illustrate points made in the text, some of the examples included are relatively unusual, and so they do not necessarily represent the norm.

'About' boxes

These boxes contain succinct information on many of the burning issues that teachers have, regarding inspection.

Author's note

Any advice given in this book concerning the health of a reader is for information and guidance only, and is not intended to replace the advice of a qualified healthcare practitioner. Symptoms of stress, in particular, require extremely careful management, and while self-treatment can help tremendously, it is always wise to have such symptoms registered with your chosen healthcare provider. Neither the author nor the publisher can be held responsible for any consequences that occur as a result of following the guidance contained herein.

CHAPTER 1

Ofsted: background and inspection personnel

Introduction

The Office for Standards in Education (Ofsted) is officially the Office of Her Majesty's Chief Inspector of Schools in England. It was set up on September 1st, 1992. Being independent from the Department for Education and Employment, and any other government department, Ofsted is non-ministerial.

The Education (Schools) Act of 1992 defines the independent system of school inspection. Ofsted's remit is to manage and administer this system. HM Inspectors (HMI)[1] are the permanent inspection staff of Ofsted. As well as playing key roles in inspecting and reporting on schools (see page 3 [HB1]), HMI also inspect independent schools (on behalf of the DfEE), teacher training and local education authority services.

Much of the work of HMI responds to requests from the Secretary of State for Education or Her Majesty's Chief Inspector. It can involve reporting on current education issues, the identification of current trends, or the evaluation of educational policy.

In September 1993, the first inspections in secondary schools took place, followed one year later by inspections in primary and special schools, and in Autumn 1996 by inspections of Pupil Referral Units. By July 1998, all schools had been inspected at least once.

Inspection personnel: who does what?

Independent inspectors carry out inspections, with the contract for inspection having been won by competitive tendering on a value-for-money basis. Ofsted is responsible for administering the contracts for inspection and determining the 'inspection window' for each school.

The inspection window is a five-week period during the school year in which an inspection may take place. Dates are finalised as a result of consultation with your school's appropriate body (usually the governing body).

ABOUT

THE POLITICAL CONTEXT OF OFSTED

In the National Association of School Masters and Women Teachers (NASUWT) Report to Conference 2000 on Ofsted inspections, the political context of Ofsted was described as follows:

'The work of Ofsted must be seen in the context of a politically driven agenda, which promotes a more rigid and complete central control over schools than was previously the case under HMI.

'Ofsted strengthens central government control over schools and diminishes the authority of local education authorities. The substantive content of education is regulated through the National Curriculum and other mandatory and non-mandatory devices, and enforced by Ofsted' (inasmuch as non-compliance would normally be reported on and highlighted for development).

Ofsted remains a key government policy for improvement in educational standards, through reporting on the strengths and development needs of individual schools. It has an extensive database of inspection reports and findings of HMI which it uses as a basis for giving advice to the Secretary of State for Education and Employment, and any other government departments and public bodies with an interest in schools, standards or other education issues.

The contractor for each inspection must set up a team of inspectors with the knowledge and expertise that reflects the specification for inspection (this is set out by Ofsted as a result of consultations with the school's appropriate authority – usually the governing body). Only contractors which meet the Quality Assurance Standard are eligible to tender for inspections (for more information, see 'Expected standards of inspectors' below).

All inspectors are trained to Ofsted standards to inspect schools. Ofsted maintains a register of inspectors who lead inspections, and a separate list of enrolled inspectors who can be part of an inspection team. A sample of inspections is checked by Ofsted as part of its quality assurance. During 1998–99, HMI was present at 30 per cent of inspections in order to check the standards and quality of inspection being offered to schools. Of the 30 per cent, 98 per cent passed.

While HMI has the task of inspecting inspectors, The House of Commons Select Committee on Education inspects Ofsted itself. About twice a year, this committee has Ofsted in its sights and there are clear lines of accountability.

There are four categories of independent inspector (i.e. those inspectors that are not on the staff of Ofsted):

1 **Registered Inspectors (RgI)** are legally responsible for conducting the inspection of a school. These responsibilities extend to the selection and deployment of the rest of the inspection team and the resulting report. RgIs are the ones in charge, carrying responsibility for almost everything to do with an inspection.

2 **Team Inspectors** are given the task of inspecting particular aspects of the work of a school, such as individual National Curriculum subjects or a year group. Their findings are contributed to the final report.

3 **Lay Inspectors**, by definition, must have 'no personal experience of any significance in the management of any school or the provision of education in any school (except as a governor or acting in any other voluntary capacity)[2]. There must be at least one lay inspector on every team.

4   **Registered Nursery Inspectors (RgNI)** are responsible, single-handedly, for the inspection of, and reporting on, funded nursery education.

● Only team and lay inspectors who have been enrolled are eligible to be inspection team members (see 'Expected standards of inspectors' below).

● Inspection teams vary in size, from 2 to about 15 inspectors.

● No member of an inspection team can have any connection (that would impede impartiality) with the school being inspected.

● Each team must appoint one or more inspectors to co-ordinate the inspection of:

    – equal opportunities;
    – special educational needs;
    – the education of pupils in the foundation stage (if relevant);
    – the education of pupils with English as an additional language (if relevant).

● If your school is a special school, the inspection team must be able to *'inspect the main types of disability represented in the school, as well as the subjects taught across the age range'*[3].

Expected standards of inspectors

The standards expected of inspectors are laid out first and foremost in the Quality Assurance Standard that is required of contractors. The Ofsted handbook *Making the Most of Inspection*[4] explains that the Quality Assurance Standard requires that:

1   Inspectors are appropriately qualified, experienced and trained to inspect the school; they have no connection with the school such that would undermine their objectivity.

2   Before the inspection starts, the lead inspector talks to the staff, explains the inspection process and answers questions, and meets with parents to seek their views of the school; the team is familiar with the context of the school and has read the relevant school documents.

3   Inspectors establish positive relationships with staff, pupils and governors. They observe lessons, look at pupils' previous work and talk

to pupils; they discuss aspects of the work of the school with members of staff and listen to their views.

4 Inspectors provide clear developmental feedback on all the judgements they have made; individual teachers are given feedback on their teaching and the co-ordination tasks they undertake; the evidence used in order to reach judgements is clear and there is an opportunity for discussion.

5 The report clearly states the judgements made and reflects what was conveyed to staff orally at the end of the inspection.

Inspectors are required to follow a Code of Conduct laid out in the Ofsted publication *Inspecting Schools: The Framework*. This states that inspectors must:

● Evaluate the work of the school objectively, be impartial and have no previous connection with the school, its staff or governors, which could undermine their objectivity.

● Report honestly and fairly, ensuring that judgements reflect accurately and reliably what the school achieves and does.

● Carry out their work with integrity, treating all those they meet with courtesy and sensitivity.

● Do all they can to minimise stress, in particular by ensuring that no teacher is over-inspected and by not asking for paperwork to be specifically prepared for the inspection.

● Act with the best interests and well-being of pupils and staff as priorities.

● Maintain purposeful and productive dialogue with staff, and communicate judgements of teachers' and the schools' work, clearly and frankly.

● Respect the confidentiality of information, particularly about teachers and the judgements made about their individual teaching.

The registered inspector and contractor are responsible for ensuring that inspection teams abide by the Code of Conduct.

Furthermore, Ofsted has made the following guarantee to teachers in an attempt to ensure that the inevitable stress of being inspected is not unnecessarily inflated:

- *'Inspectors will do everything possible to work with you in keeping the stress of an inspection to a minimum;*
- *Inspectors will not expect you to create additional paperwork specifically for the inspection;*
- *Inspectors will always treat you in a courteous and friendly manner, particularly when entering and leaving your classroom;*
- *Normally, you will be observed for no more than half of any one day, and never more than three-quarters;*
- *Inspectors will not judge teaching unless they have observed a significant part of the lesson, normally for at least 30 minutes;*
- *Inspectors will use confidential information responsibly;*
- *Inspectors will discuss important aspects of your teaching with you;*
- *Inspectors will explain the reasons for their judgements and be helpful in identifying where improvement is needed.'* [5]

In addition to the guarantee and Quality Assurance Standard and the Code of Conduct, the *Handbooks for Inspecting Schools* also make explicit the standards expected of inspectors, by stating that:

'A good inspection is one where:

- *judgements about the educational standards achieved at the school, and the strengths and weaknesses in teaching and other aspects, are secured by sufficient, valid and reliable evidence;*
- *the main findings, summarised at the front of the inspection report, together with issues which the school should address in order to improve, are clearly identified and reported to the school.'*

The *Handbooks* go on to explain to inspectors that:

'It is equally important that:

- *inspectors establish an effective working relationship with the school based on professionalism, sensitivity and an understanding of the school's concerns and circumstances;*
- *the process of inspection is well planned and effectively managed;*

THE SKILLS OF INDIVIDUAL INSPECTORS

❯ From talking to teachers who have experienced inspection, inspectors themselves, and from the feedback on inspection given to organisations such as OFSTIN (see below) and teaching unions, there are tremendous differences in the skills of individual inspectors. The way in which teachers and managers perceive an inspection must be partly attributable to the way that inspectors conduct themselves whilst in schools. However, all human interactions require at least an element of empathy from all participants, if real progress is to be the result of the interaction.

❯ It is an unfortunate fact of life that, just as not all teachers perform to exactly the same high standards at all times (the same can be said of doctors, dentists, pilots, politicians, etc.), not all inspectors are perfectly faultless! If you experience an inspection during which an inspector clearly does not have the skills required to perform his/her duties, it is essential that you make your views known. See pages 89–93 for information on making complaints about an inspector or an inspection.

- *there are good communications with the school and individual staff, which lead to a clear and shared understanding of what is involved at each stage of the inspection;*
- *inspectors readily explore issues with staff through professional dialogue;*
- *feedback to the school, staff and the governing body, both orally and in writing, is clear and comprehensible.'* [6]

There is no doubt that inspectors are expected to leave staff with a sense of having gained from the experience of being inspected. In addition to this, they should ensure, through actions and words, that staff appreciate the thoroughness of the evidence base from which judgements have emerged.

From the accumulation of these expected standards, it is clear that inspectors have an immense responsibility to ensure that any inspection passes without undue stress and with maximised chances of the school gaining as much as possible from the experience. Above all, in the publication *Inspecting Schools, The Framework*, inspectors are told that they must '*inspire confidence in their work and their judgements, and create a climate in which the inspection process makes a valuable contribution to improvement*'.

If you have any concerns about the conduct of your inspection, it is essential that you raise them with the appropriate people.

ABOUT

OFSTIN

The Office for Standards in Inspection (OFSTIN) was founded by a group of unfunded educators to focus on possible alternatives to the current system of inspection. As a result of a commissioned independent review, a national conference and various regional seminars, OFSTIN has called for certain changes to be made. To find out more about OFSTIN, see Useful Addresses (page 225 [HB4]) for contact details.

1   HM Inspectors were originally established in 1839.

2   Ofsted Corporate Plan 1999

3   *Inspecting Schools, The Framework*, Ofsted, 1999.

4   Ofsted, 1998.

5   *Inspecting Schools, The Framework*, Ofsted, 1998.

6   *The Handbooks for Inspecting Schools*, TSO, 1999.

CHAPTER 2

School inspection:
what is it about?

'There is nothing you cannot do if you keep calm and go forward.'
WHOOPI GOLDBERG

In the Teacherline[1] First Report, published in May 2000, Ofsted inspections were cited as the main cause of stress in eight per cent of calls where stress was an issue. Of these calls, a number indicated 'a lack of understanding of the process of inspections, and suggested a shared conspiracy of silence'. The Report goes on to explain that it was fear of showing vulnerability or weakness that prevented most teachers from seeking support from colleagues and managers on the finer details of an impending inspection. The following section seeks to address this situation.

Purposes of school inspection

The most basic purpose of school inspection is to help teachers to improve standards, through an entire, external evaluation of the work of schools. This has a natural knock-on effect in the creation of sub-purposes, such as the encouragement of ongoing, internal self-review and public identification of excellent and struggling schools (adding to the information previously available to parents and taxpayers on what is going on in schools).

According to the Ofsted booklet *Making the Most of Inspection*, inspection should provide schools with '*an independent assessment of what you need to know: how well your school is doing, what strengths and weaknesses there are, and what needs to improve*'.[2]

Through the gathering of such detailed information on schools, a national database of educational standards now exists and is being used in informing education policies, as well as providing a management tool for headteachers, governors and local education authorities.

While inspection in itself cannot raise standards, the goal is that standards will be raised, supported and maintained *through and as a result of* inspection.

Types of inspection

There are two types of inspection carried out by teams of inspectors under the authority of Ofsted. The latter has a legislative duty to ensure that inspections are carried out on the following types of school at least once every six years:

- Community schools
- Foundation schools
- Voluntary aided schools
- Voluntary controlled schools
- City technology colleges
- City colleges for the technology of the arts
- Community special schools
- Foundation special schools
- Pupil referral units
- Non-maintained special schools
- Maintained nursery schools

Full inspection

The full inspection is what the majority of teachers experience during their careers. The aspects of a school's functioning, listed in the Evaluation Schedule (see pages 21–54), are inspected and reported on; and individual teachers receive a profile of inspectors' judgements on

---

their work, as well as verbal feedback either during or at the end of an inspection. This is in accordance with the School Inspections Act 1996, which states that inspectors must report on:

• Educational standards in the school.
• The quality of education provided.
• The management of financial resources.
• The spiritual, moral, social and cultural development of pupils.

Short inspection

This inspection is designed for schools already deemed to be most effective and should be regarded more as a 'check up' rather than a full-blown 'medical'. They are shorter than full inspections (usually lasting two or three days), and often fewer inspectors are involved, as not all teachers are observed. The inspection team is led by a registered inspector.

As with full inspections, short inspections also report on standards, achievements, efficiency of financial management and the spiritual, moral, social and cultural development of pupils, but they do not report on each subject in detail.

If, for any reason, the school is deemed to be underachieving following a short inspection, it will be closely monitored (by Her Majesty's Inspectors, HMI), or will face a full Ofsted inspection in the (possibly near) future. Generally, short inspections are thought to place less pressure on schools than full inspections.

Ofsted uses a combination of four main factors when deciding whether a school should have a full or a short inspection. Therefore, if your school has '*a favourable report from the last inspection; a record of improvement (or sustained high standards); favourable achievements in relation to similar schools; and good performance in relation to national averages*'[3], there is a fairly high chance that just a short inspection will be necessary.

FACING A SHORT INSPECTION

❯ If your school has been notified that it is to receive a short inspection, it is helpful to be aware that, although you may not be observed, you should prepare as though you are going to be! Also, be aware that you will probably have less time to demonstrate or discuss exactly what you can do. There is likely to be a focus on literacy and numeracy in your school, and co-ordinators for these curriculum areas should at least expect to be interviewed.

❯ Remaining core-subject co-ordinators/managers may also be interviewed.

❯ Short inspections are in their infancy, but certain patterns seem to be emerging from those schools that have received one, not least that at primary level, year six appears to be receiving particular attention, and there seems to be a heightened focus on the spiritual, moral, social and cultural aspects of the education on offer. However, these are just observations and should not be taken as Ofsted policy. At the end of a short inspection, your performance will not be graded and you may not even receive any verbal feedback, especially if your observed lesson was deemed to be satisfactory or above. During short inspections, inspectors may not wait to observe a whole lesson.

❯ Inspectors have the same standards and Code of Conduct to adhere to when performing a short inspection. Thus, the advice on making complaints, should the need arise, applies equally to short and full inspections.

Advantages and disadvantages of inspection

It has often been said that with the right planning and organisation (not to mention perspective!), an inspection should offer long-term advantages that outweigh any disadvantages. Unfortunately, this is not the experience of all teachers in all schools.

Tables 2.1 and 2.2 are the end-result of extensive conversations with teachers and inspectors. They summarise what are seen as the main advantages and disadvantages, respectively, of inspection as a concept. It can be very useful to ponder these points prior to an inspection, to help minimise the chance of any disadvantages that you may suffer obliterating your view of any advantages that can be gained.

The tables are by no means definitive, and the points they contain are in no significant order.

Table 2.1: Advantages of a system of inspection

Encourages a focus on public accountability issues.
Knowledge and skills can be recognised.
Can be confidence building – a boost for all staff, bring them together in a common purpose.
Can encourage further development of skills, in particular improved management systems – in short, it may be a catalyst for change.
Focuses the mind on what is working and what is not, encouraging self-review and peer review through the examination of content and delivery of lessons.
Can inspire organisation of the physical environment.
Findings can affirm the direction that a school is taking, or illuminate future direction(s).
Evidence of good work and achievements can be made public.
Relationships between colleagues can flourish through the human grace needed when a team is under scrutiny.
Can question security, which may lead to a positive/creative response.
Can be empowering if a commitment to change is needed and then harnessed.
Can highlight change over time.
Use of an inspection system means that other methods of success measurement, such as educational output, are not solely relied upon.
Teachers often work in a 'sealed-off' environment. Inspections can break that isolation in schools that do not carry out peer observations.

Table 2.2: Disadvantages of a system of inspection

Can create tremendous crescendos for staff to deal with, regardless of outcome.
Can cause unnecessary fear, often of the unknown and unknowable.
Inspection can sap energy from a school, leading to a rise in staff sickness rates.
Any criticism delivered can be perceived as harsh rather than developmental and supportive, particularly if the merits of alternative approaches to school effectiveness have not been recognised.
Can cause negative stress with far-reaching – and sometimes devastating – effects.
The additional workload involved may add to the pressure felt by an already stretched team.
The findings may simply be an affirmation of what is already known by the school.
The public nature of inspections may add to the pressure felt by the school's staff, and inspections may even be viewed as punitive.
Inspections can focus too much on outcome and not enough on process.
Can question security, which may lead to a negative/destructive response.
Can be difficult to determine the link between inspection and improvement.
Can be seen as irrelevant in a school that is accomplished at self-review.
The professional skills of inspection personnel can vary tremendously, and no system can be fully objective.
Some teachers prefer to safeguard their privacy and do not thrive on exposing their work.

Strengths and weaknesses

There would be very little point in inspecting a school specifically to uncover weaknesses, regardless of any strengths that may exist. That said, there would also be little point in going through an inspection only to be told that you are doing well, with no regard to what aspects might be improved.

The language involved in the assessment of what a school is doing well and what needs improvement seems to have taken on new meaning in the context of inspection, and this has not always been useful to teachers.

In the process of establishing a judgement on the quality of education that is delivered at your school, inspectors will identify key strengths (i.e. what your school is doing well) and key weaknesses (or development needs).

Perhaps it is a reflection of human nature that we tend to cling onto 'weaknesses' as the defining features of our work, while glossing over our positive achievements. Whatever the nature of the development needs that are highlighted as a result of an inspection in your school, always keep in mind that those needs cannot be met without the commitment of everyone involved. Improvement is not something that can be achieved single-handedly by any one member of your school's community; likewise, individuals should not feel the burden of responsibility for the *need* for improvement, either.

How judgements are made

The judgements made on your school will be drawn from an *evidence base* that will have been compiled by your Registered Inspector. This evidence base must be kept for at least 12 months after the inspection, in case it needs to be re-examined.

Before the inspectors arrive at your school, they will have compiled a *pre-inspection commentary*. This consists of evidence they have gathered to date from the information available to them, which includes:

1 The Pre-Inspection Context and School Indicator (PICSI) Report, provided by Ofsted.

2 The Performance and Assessment (PANDA) Report.

3 Forms completed by your school before inspection, and any other documentation from your school.

4 Previous inspection reports and subsequent action plans.

5 The information given to inspectors by parents at the parents' meeting, and through the questionnaire for parents (it is not compulsory for schools to send parents a questionnaire, but it has certainly come to be expected).

6 Discussions with your headteacher and anyone else that inspectors may have met on pre-inspection visits.

The forms that will have been completed by your school before inspection are:

➤ S1 (consultation about the inspection and information about your school);

➤ S2 (information about your school);

➤ S3 (your school's self-audit); and

➤ S4 (your headteacher's statement).

The Pre-Inspection Commentary outlines the general characteristics of your school. The aim is that it will give the entire inspection team a solid background into what type of school yours is and how it is performing. Perhaps most significantly, this Commentary will record the initial hypotheses about your school that your inspectors will be testing. The Commentary will record comments under the main headings of the Evaluation Schedule (see page 21).

Once the inspection has begun, the evidence base from which inspectors draw their conclusions expands further. During lesson observations they will complete *evidence forms* and record grades that reflect judgements on teaching and learning, attainment and attitudes, and behaviour. These grades run from 0–7 and can be interpreted as follows:

0 Insufficient evidence to form a judgement

1 Excellent

2 Very good (favourable, well above average, promotes very high standards and quality)

3 Good

4 Satisfactory (broadly typical, average, promotes sound standards and quality)

5 Unsatisfactory

6 Poor (unfavourable, well below average, promotes very low standards and quality)

7 Very poor

During a full inspection, all inspectors must complete an *Inspection Notebook*. In it, the inspector must record strengths and weaknesses, and any other judgements that s/he has made. During short inspections, inspectors may, but do not have to, complete an Inspection Notebook.

The judgements made in the Inspection Notebook must be based on evidence, and the source of that evidence must be made explicit. The Notebook focuses inspectors mainly on the Evaluation Schedule, a summary of their lesson observations, and main points that they may have for discussion and feedback, concentrating on your school's strengths and weaknesses.

Do be aware that it is not simply through lesson observations that judgements are formed. Inspectors may also talk to teachers, governors, pupils, non-teaching staff and parents. Such 'informal chats' may influence conclusions that are drawn.

The *Record of Corporate Judgements* made by your inspection team is another factor in the inspectors' evidence base. It records findings along the lines of the Evaluation Schedule:

- The strengths and weaknesses that inspectors have identified, along with the sources for their evidence;
- The grades that inspectors have given in each section of the Evaluation Schedule;
- The improvements that your school needs to make;
- Whether the inspection team feels your school requires *special measures* (see pages 193–7) or is deemed to have serious weaknesses;
- The evidence base that has been used for inspection.

Teacher accountability

To whom and to what teachers are accountable cannot easily be answered. It would seem that teachers must follow the steps of a complex dance, the tune to which may be provided by their leaders, headteacher, governors, local education authority, parents, pupils, inspectors and Ofsted, the Qualifications and Curriculum Authority (QCA), the Teacher Training Agency (TTA) and the Government. This should be a tune of beautiful harmony, but occasionally what results is a cacophony.

Ofsted inspections focus the minds of teachers and parents on national and local accountability, and not least on the fact that schools are a public service using a tremendous amount of public money (an annual budget of around £18 billion). This focus is heightened by the publication of a written report on each school.

The fact that accountability is a necessary part of professional life is not in question, but knowing who you, as a teacher, are accountable to, is. Accountability appears to have a symbolic meaning separate from its literal meaning, and this symbolism can strike fear at the hearts of even the most conscientious of teachers. In fact, it is often such teachers that suffer most at the hands of their own self-doubt and self-criticism, seeing accountability either as a regulatory mechanism, or as something that needs to be externally applied in order for them to perform their duties to acceptable standards. However, accountability should not force you to define your practice defensively; if anything, it should encourage a positive response in providing clarity and transparency in your work to all those you are working for.

For the purposes of inspection, do not focus on the wider (public) picture of accountability. Simply follow the guidance of your managers and leaders, and think no further than your immediate accountability (with pupils in mind) to your headteacher and governors. When your school is undergoing an inspection, your accountability does not change. Inspectors do not assume a place in the hierarchy of your school's management, and so within your school you remain accountable to those that you work with – be they managers, leaders, your headteacher or colleagues.

In every school, there is a *process* of accountability that can only be accepted and respected if the expectations made of teachers are clear in their boundaries and parameters.

ABOUT

WHAT INSPECTION IS *NOT*

❯ It is important to give thought to what an inspection is not, if only to encourage and nurture perspective. It has often been said, but needs to be stated again, that inspection is a 'snapshot' of your work as a teacher at that time. It does not define or delineate your future career, and does not place restrictions on the scope of your future development as a teacher. Indeed, the week following the publication of your inspection report will probably see it going out of date, if you work in a dynamic institution that responds to the changing needs of its members. This is because what is written will relate to what was happening in your school during the time of the inspection.

❯ Inspection cannot simply be a faultfinding exercise, and the judgements made (particularly the less favourable ones) should not be worn by teachers for eternity! For inspection to be most useful to schools and their pupils, teachers must be able to take from judgements what will promote development, and shake off anything else.

1   Teacherline is the national counselling, support and advice service for teachers. 24-hour freephone: 0800 0562 561. First Report *Managing Stress in Schools* by Patrick Nash.

2   *Making the Most of Inspection*, Ofsted, 1998.

3   *Inspecting Schools, The Framework*, Ofsted, January 2000.

CHAPTER 3

The Evaluation Schedule:
what is inspected?

The Evaluation Schedule sets out for inspectors (and teachers) the sequence for evaluation of the school. It also defines the summary of the final report. Being familiar with the Schedule can really help to remove the mystery from what inspectors are actually doing when they visit your classroom, as well as giving you a feel for what aspects of the inspection you can impact and what aspects you cannot!

There are five main elements to the Evaluation Schedule as defined in the *Handbooks for Inspecting Schools*, broken down into eight main sub-sections. These are discussed individually, in some detail, herein:

Context and Overview

What sort of school is it?

Outcomes

How high are standards?

a) The school's results and pupils' achievements

b) Pupils' attitudes, values and personal development

Quality of Provision

How well are pupils taught?

How good are the curricular and other opportunities offered to pupils?

How well does the school care for its pupils?

How well does the school work in partnership with parents?

Efficiency and Effectiveness of Management

How well is the school led and managed?

Issues for the School

What should the school do to improve further?

Inspectors also evaluate and report on any additional features for inspection, and the standards and quality of teaching in areas of the curriculum, subjects and courses.

The Handbooks for Inspecting Schools [1] explain what inspectors must assess and report on in each section of the Evaluation Schedule. Your school may well have a copy of the relevant *Handbook,* and it is worth looking through it for information on how inspectors will be using the Evaluation Schedule. There are numerous benefits to be had from becoming familiar with what inspectors will be focusing and reporting on when inspecting your school.

Most importantly, this kind of preparation will:

- Enable you to prepare mentally for inspection – knowledge can help to eliminate fear of the unknown.

- Enable you to make explicit the evidence that inspectors will be seeking.

- Assist you in preparing pupils for inspection.

- Eliminate speculation as to what inspectors do *not* look for.

ABOUT

THE EVALUATION SCHEDULE

❯ While it is rarely a wise idea to 'teach/learn to the exam', there is something to be said for becoming familiar with the focus of an inspection.

❯ Furthermore, aiming to incorporate key aspects of the Evaluation Schedule into your daily cycle of planning, even when there is no sign of an impending inspection, can encourage the habit of self-review and self-evaluation.

❯ However, do acknowledge the fact that many teachers are already incorporating the main elements of the Evaluation Schedule in their daily work. Please do not read on feeling that there is so much to do; you may already be doing it!

The guidance given to inspectors on using the Evaluation Schedule has been summarised above. For further information, you may like to refer to the *Handbooks for Inspecting Schools.*

The above eight sub-sections are discussed in some detail subsequently.

What sort of school is it?

Inspectors must report on the characteristics of the school, and evaluate and summarise:

- The effectiveness of the school, including the value for money it provides;
- The main strengths and weaknesses of the school;
- The extent to which the school has improved, or not, since the last inspection.

The findings of inspectors must relate to the specific nature of the school and its pupils.

This means that inspectors will be looking at:

▶ Whether your school is like other schools (in terms of number, gender and age of pupils, type of school, and the status of subscription to your school).

▶ What pupils have attained on entry to your school (if this information is known).

▶ Whether your school has a specific designation, such as 'centre of excellence' or 'beacon school'.

▶ The location of your school, whether the intake reflects the immediate surroundings, and background of its pupils.

▶ The proportion of pupils eligible for free school meals.

▶ Different groups reflected in your school's population (for example, traveller children, ethnic groups, pupils with special educational needs, etc.).

Inspectors must also judge the effectiveness of your school. In order to do this, they will base their conclusions on:

- the standards that pupils achieve;
- the quality of education that your school provides;
- the quality of leadership and management in your school;
- the improvements that your school has made or maintained since its last inspection.

Although all aspects of your school's effectiveness will be scrutinised, there is no doubt that the achievement of pupils carries significant importance.

Inspectors are given an aid to judge the effectiveness of schools, based on a seven-point grading system where 1 is deemed to be 'excellent' and 7 is deemed to be 'very poor' (Table 3.1).

Table 3.1: Evaluation judgement record: grading system

Judgement recording grade	1	2	3	4	5	6	7
Standards							
Pupils' achievements are: Excellent	*	*	*	*	*	Very poor	
Attitudes, values and personal developments are: Excellent						Very poor	
Provision							
The quality of education, particularly teaching, is: Excellent						Very poor	
Leadership and management							
Leadership and management are: Excellent						Very poor	
Improvement							
Improvement or maintenance of very high standard is: Excellent						Very poor	
Contextual factors							
The context of school in the local environment is: Very favourable						Very unfavourable	
Effectiveness							
The overall effectiveness of the school is: Excellent						Very poor	

As far as the first section of the Evaluation Schedule is concerned (regarding the overall effectiveness of the school), the terms 'very good' or 'excellent' will be used in either written or oral feedback if the following characteristics apply. These characteristics assist inspectors in pitching their judgements – they are not set in stone:

The school achieves the highest standards possible in most of its work. High proportions of pupils are keen to learn. There are no significant problems of behaviour or absenteeism. The teaching is consistently good, with much that is very good; and virtually all pupils progress well. The staff constantly look for ways to improve the quality of their teaching, are imaginative and make challenging demands of pupils. There are very good arrangements to support all pupils and care for them, and the school has a strong partnership with parents and carers. The school is well governed and self-critical. It knows what is does well, where its weaknesses are and how to improve them. It has made significant improvements since its last inspection or has sustained high standards. It provides good or very good value for money[2].

The following characteristics describe a school deemed to be 'satis-factory' or better:

The school achieves standards that are at least as good as they should be. Pupils have good attitudes. Almost all the teaching is at least satisfactory and much is good or better, and pupils are learning well. The school has developed a curriculum that meets the needs of individual pupils and provides opportunities which benefit all pupils. There are sound care arrangements. The school keeps parents and carers informed about their child's progress and enlists their support. The school has made satisfactory improvements since its last inspection and responds adequately to the challenges or issues it faces. It is inclusive in its policies, outlook and practices, and is led and managed in a cost-effective way, providing at least satisfactory value for money.[3]

The extent to which your school *does not* fall into these two cate-gories (very good or excellent, or satisfactory or better) determines whether it is deemed to be 'poor', 'very poor' or 'failing'.

ACTION: *If you are facing an inspection in your school, take a minute or two to think about these characteristics of overall effectiveness. Try not to make instant judgements on your performance or that of your school as a whole, but aim to become familiar with what is deemed to contribute to 'success'.*

When the inspection team has its final meeting, it has to decide what the school does well and what could be improved. The advice to inspectors when focusing on these issues is that their judgements must truly reflect the school and the quality of education that it offers.

Now that all schools have been inspected at least once, inspectors have the unenviable task of assessing the extent to which each school has improved since its last inspection. This is not as arbitrary as it could be, because five factors must be considered by the inspectors:

1 The change that can be *reasonably* expected.

2 Exactly what the school has done to improve and whether that can be deemed to be sufficient.

3 The evidence for improvement that can be drawn from trends in standards in, for example, the core National Curriculum subjects.

4 What observations have been made of improvements in the quality of teaching and learning (particularly in areas deemed to be 'weak').

5 How well the school's management has responded to the previous inspection.

How high are the standards?

There are two elements to the assessment of standards in a school:

a The school's results and pupils' achievements;

b Pupils' attitudes, values and personal development.

The school's results and pupils' achievements

Results and achievements have to be *interpreted* and *evaluated* by inspectors. This, among other things, means looking at:

- Performance data for the end of each keystage (with the emphasis on English, mathematics and science).

- Performance trends over time.

- Progress towards targets.

- Standards of work seen (with emphasis on literacy and numeracy, but with the expectation of consistent standards across the curriculum. It is worth being aware that, although literacy and numeracy receives what could be described as 'special attention', inspectors will draw evidence for their conclusions on pupil competency from across the entire curriculum).

- The achievement of pupils and the demands placed on them.

Standards can be related to clear benchmarks, such as National Curriculum level descriptors, but will also be applied to broader characteristics of a school such as pupil attitudes and behaviour.

Achievement seems to be slightly more problematic for inspectors. While being advised that achievement can reflect '*what you would expect of those particular pupils*', inspectors are advised that '*reference to terms such as 'ability' or 'aptitude' requires caution, for it is questionable what evidence you will have of such attributes*'.[4]

Thus, as well as analysing your school's performance data, inspectors will also have to satisfy themselves, while in your school, that they have determined what pupils can do, understand and know. This means that when they visit your classroom, they will also want to determine:

- whether pupils can apply their knowledge to related problems;
- whether pupils are suitably challenged;
- the standard and extent of work already achieved.

This is not done without consideration of these factors:

- Identified special educational needs;
- Possible frequent changes of school experienced by pupils;
- Ethnic minority pupils, such as asylum seekers and refugees;
- The possibility that English as a second or other language might block the progress of affected pupils.

The *Handbooks for Inspecting Schools* suggest results as being 'very high or excellent' in primary schools if:

Results are well above average or almost all pupils are on course to meet or exceed: learning goals by the end of Reception; National Curriculum Level 2 in English, Mathematics or Science by 7; and Level 4 by 11 years. Standards of literacy and numeracy are very high.

And in secondary schools if:

Results are well above average or almost all pupils are on course to meet or exceed expected standards in English, Mathematics and Science by 14 and 16 and standards appropriate to the course at post-16. Standards of literacy and numeracy are very high.

The *Handbooks* also suggest results as being 'sound or better' in both primary and secondary schools if:

Results are at least average, compared with all other schools and current work indicates standards are rising. Standards in literacy and numeracy are adequate for work in other subjects. Standards in other subjects of the National Curriculum are usually sound for pupils of the particular age.

Achievements are thought to be 'very high or excellent' in primary schools if:

Most pupils are working at or near their capacity and achieving well in terms of their earlier attainment. Standards are higher than in similar schools and work in lessons is demanding. There is much added value.

And in secondary schools if:

Most pupils are working at or near their capacity and achieving well in terms of: earlier achievement; value added measures and comparisons with other schools.

Achievements are thought to be 'sound or better' in primary schools if:

Pupils are making satisfactory progress and achieving at least as well as in most similar schools. Almost all teaching is at least satisfactory but there is scope for greater challenge.

And in secondary schools if:

Pupils are making satisfactory progress and achieving as much as could be expected, some of them more. The school is achieving at least as well as most similar schools.

Anything that falls below these descriptors is unlikely to be satisfactory.

Trends in results over time will also be looked at, in particular:

● Improvements in your school compared with all schools;

- Whether performance in all subjects is consistent;
- The performance of girls in relation to boys and whether that deviates from what is found nationally;
- Whether particular groups of pupils perform differently from the remainder of your school's population.

Pupils' attitudes, values and personal development

An enormous task, but inspectors must evaluate and report on:
- Attitudes to your school;
- The incidence of exclusions and behaviour in general;
- Personal development of pupils and their relationships;
- Attendance.

This means that when they are in your school, inspectors will be observing:
- how keen pupils are to be at school;
- how responsive they are to the activities of your school and school life in general;
- how pupils behave in lessons and around the school generally;
- any bullying, racism or sexism that may be apparent;
- how well pupils are able to reflect on their behaviour and its impact;
- how respectful pupils are of the feelings, values and beliefs of others;
- how willing pupils are to take responsibility and demonstrate initiative;
- attendance, and levels of unauthorised absence.

In short, inspectors will need to assess how pupils respond to what is provided for them. This does not only refer to teaching, but to the examples set by staff and the way in which your school nurtures spiritual, moral, social and cultural development. This will be achieved not only through observation, but also through discussions with pupils.

According to the *Handbook for Inspecting Primary and Nursery Schools*[5], the attitudes, values and personal development of pupils may be deemed to be 'very good or excellent' if these characteristics apply:

Pupils are eager to come to school and are quickly and positively involved in a wide range of activities. They behave very well in and around the school, and work constructively and co-operatively in groups and productively on their own. They enjoy learning and are reluctant to stop when they have to. Pupils are tolerant of each other, and show a mature and growing understanding of each other and of different viewpoints. Behaviour and punctuality are excellent. The attendance figures for the school are at or above the national average, and there are no exclusions.

'Satisfactory or better' has these characteristics:
Most pupils like school and the youngest are mainly confident in leaving their parents or carers. They are willing to help each other, teachers and other adults and take part in activities outside lessons. Most pupils behave well most of the time and they are able to work on their own. Pupils are kind and considerate and show an increasing respect for each other and a willingness to listen. They are punctual to lessons and rarely absent.

If inspectors witness 'more than isolated' incidents of unruliness, aggressive behaviour, racism or sexism, attitudes, values and personal development will probably be assessed as being less than satisfactory.

According to the *Handbook for Inspecting Secondary Schools* [6], the attitudes, values and personal development of pupils will be deemed to be 'very good or excellent' if these characteristics apply:
Pupils and students are keen to come to school and are quickly and positively involved in a wide range of activities. They make the most of the opportunities provided. They behave very well in and around the school, and work constructively and co-operatively in groups and productively on their own. Pupils and students have respect for each other, and show a very mature understanding of each other and of different viewpoints. Misbehaviour is very rare, punctuality is good. The attendance figures for the school are above the national average and attendance in years 10 and 11 is good. Exclusions are very low for this type of school.

'Satisfactory or better' has these characteristics in secondary schools:

Most pupils like, or at least accept, school. They are willing to help each other and their teachers and take part in activities outside lessons. Their behaviour is good most of the time and they are able, and can be relied on, to work on their own. Pupils are kind and considerate and show respect for each other and a willingness to listen. They are mainly punctual to lessons and rarely absent. Exclusions are low.

Again, if inspectors witness '*more than isolated*' incidents of unruliness, aggressive behaviour, truancy, poor punctuality, racism or sexism, attitudes, values and personal development will probably be assessed as being less than satisfactory.

This means that inspectors will be looking out for (among others) the extent to which:

❯ Pupils know what is expected of them and are involved in your school's routines and organisation.

❯ Pupils are willing to act on their initiative.

❯ Pupils demonstrate a willingness to help and support each other, building constructive relationships.

❯ Pupils can reflect on their behaviour and understand the impact of what they do.

❯ Pupils are prepared to be open to the influences of reasoned argument.

❯ The teaching in your school interests pupils.

❯ The quality of links between your school and pupils' homes.

❯ Pupils can plan and organise work when necessary.

❯ Pupils develop and demonstrate confidence.

❯ The importance that your school places on the cultural and other values of its pupils, and that your pupils place on those of others.

❯ Pupils feel part of your school's community.

How well are pupils taught?

Probably the area of inspection that can stress teachers the most. This is where inspectors can get right behind the methods you adopt in the delivery of the National Curriculum, why you adopt them and what the result is.

During an inspection, inspectors must evaluate:

- The quality of your teaching, what impact it has on learning in your classroom and how successful your teaching is;
- How well you teach literacy and numeracy skills;
- The extent to which your teaching meets the needs of *all* your pupils;
- The extent to which pupils actually learn in your lessons.

This means that you will have to show inspectors that:

- Your subject knowledge is good;
- You are competent in teaching basic skills;
- Your planning reflects objectives that pupils understand;
- Your expectations of pupils are high and you seek to inspire and challenge pupils;
- Your methods of teaching facilitate effective learning and your standards for behaviour are high;
- You deploy resources such as ICT and support staff, and use the time available to you effectively;
- Through thorough assessment you bring pupils through difficulties;
- Use homework to reinforce and extend work learned.

Inspectors will also want to see that pupils:

- Are acquiring knowledge and skills;
- Can apply effort to their work, be it physical, creative or intellectual;
- Work at a good pace and are productive;
- Are interested in what they do and motivated to learn for themselves;
- Understand what they can do well and what can be improved.

Although this means that inspectors will need to scrutinise the work that goes on in your lesson, this scrutiny will probably have its base in these three elements:

1   The *context* and *relevance* of what you teach and its relation to what you have previously taught the pupils.

2   The *methods* you adopt and how you choose to *structure* the lesson.

3   What you demand of *all* the pupils and how effectively you *engage* them in their tasks.

This is a difficult challenge for even the most experienced inspector. Inspectors are expected to be able to give examples illustrating how you enable learning to take place, as well as what you might do to improve things. In order for them to reach a conclusion on what they witness as standards of teaching, they will need not only to observe you and your pupils at work, but to engage in possibly extensive discussions with you and your pupils as well. Expect pupils to be asked questions that will enable them to demonstrate the depth of understanding they have of the work they have done.

Inspectors are warned that, when they report on teaching in schools, they need to be '*crystal clear in terms of what works, what does not, why and what should be done about it*'[7]. They are also told explicitly to ensure that the messages they give on the quality of teaching in your school are consistent with the messages they give on standards and the leadership and management of the school.

According to *The Handbooks for Inspecting Schools*[8], the quality of teaching that your pupils receive could be 'very good or excellent' in primary schools if these characteristics apply:

> *The teaching of skills and subject matter is knowledgeable, stimulating and perceptive. It uses imaginative resources and makes intellectual and creative demands on pupils to extend their learning. Challenging questions are used to consolidate, extend and verify what pupils know and understand. The methods chosen are well geared to the particular focus and demands of the lesson and make*

the most productive use of the time available. Relationships in the classroom provide a confident and positive atmosphere in which achievement flourishes. Pupils are keen to learn, rise to challenges in creative ways and think further. They work well for extended periods of time and make very good progress.

'Satisfactory or better' teaching in primary schools has these characteristics:

The teaching of basic skills and subject content is clear and accurate, using clear explanation and demonstration, and involving all pupils. The organisation of the lesson allows most pupils to keep up with the work and to complete tasks in the time available. Staff interact with pupils to check their understanding and to ensure they remain on task. The relationship between the pupils and teacher is such that pupils can get on with their work and know how well they have done.

The quality of teaching that your pupils receive could be 'very good or excellent' in secondary schools if these characteristics apply:

The teaching of skills and subject matter is knowledgeable, stimulating and exciting; it uses imaginative resources and makes intellectual and creative demands on pupils to take their learning further. Challenging questions are used to consolidate, extend and verify what pupils know and understand. The methods chosen are well geared to the particular focus and demands of the lesson and make the most productive use of the time available. Relationships in the classroom provide a confident and positive atmosphere in which achievement flourishes. Pupils are keen to learn, rise to challenges in creative ways and think further. They work well for extended periods of time and as a result gains in knowledge and understanding are very high.

'Satisfactory or better' has these characteristics in secondary schools:

The teaching of basic skills and subject content is clear and accurate, using explanation and demonstration and involving all pupils. The organisation of the lesson allows most pupils to keep up with the work and to complete tasks in the time available. Teachers check pupils' understanding and ensure they remain on task. The relationship between the pupils and teacher is such that pupils can get on with their work and know how well they have done. Most pupils show sound application to work.

Teaching will not be satisfactory in both primary and secondary schools if any of the following applies:

- *'Teachers' knowledge of subjects is not good enough to promote demanding work;*
- *Basic skills are not taught effectively;*
- *A significant minority of pupils are not engaged in the lesson;*
- *Lessons are poorly planned and organised and time is wasted;*
- *There are weaknesses in controlling the class;*
- *Pupils do not know what they are doing;*
- *Pupils are not making progress.'*

In terms of making explicit the teaching skills that you have, it is wise to demonstrate as far as possible how good your subject knowledge is. Inspectors will expect to see evidence of this, not only through your lesson planning and presentation, but also through your use of resources and discussions with you.

The effectiveness of your chosen teaching methods as *demonstrated to the inspectors* will be under particular scrutiny. Where possible, aim to ensure that:

1 Your exposition captures attention as well as informs. Pay attention to its structure.

2 If you group by ability in any way, you can show that this results in higher standards.

3 Your questioning is able to challenge and engage pupils.

4 Any practical work offers pupils the opportunity to think about how it has impacted their understanding (perhaps through feedback or recapping), and they can see ways of improving their work.

5 The way in which you group pupils for work (alone, in pairs, in small groups, etc.) helps you to achieve the objectives you have set.

6 You are truly in a position to interact with as many different pupils as possible.

7 Your use of resources is balanced in comparison with the background and culture of individual pupils.

In terms of behaviour management, inspectors will need to see that, as far as possible:

- your authority is clear and fair throughout your lessons;
- your pupils' attention is held and you encourage concentration;
- pupils are organised into work efficiently;
- you can support and control pupils;
- you have created an atmosphere of mutual respect and a work habit;
- pupils know your expectations of self-discipline and mature behaviour.

How good are the curricular and other opportunities offered to pupils?

In many ways, this section is less in the direct control of individual teachers, although the influence that teachers can have on a positive assessment in this area should not be underestimated.

In order to cover the schedule, inspectors will evaluate and report on:

1 The range and quality of the opportunities for learning that your school provides. This will specifically include extra-curricular activities, personal, social and health education (PSHE), and the links your school has with the community and local schools and colleges.

2 The way in which your school meets the requirements of the National Curriculum and religious education.

3 The way in which your school cultivates the spiritual, moral, social and cultural development of pupils.

In order to reach any conclusions on these three main factors, inspectors will want to determine the extent to which your school:

- can meet the needs, aptitudes and interests of its pupils through the range of opportunities that it offers;
- teaches numeracy and literacy effectively;
- provides learning support and other extracurricular activities outside the school day;
- ensures equality of access and opportunity for all pupils;
- encourages self-knowledge, reflection and the development of spiritual awareness through knowledge and insights into values and beliefs;
- promotes the distinction between right and wrong;
- promotes the development of responsibility, initiative and an understanding of the concept of community;
- encourages an appreciation of pupils' cultural traditions and the diversity of other cultures;
- effectively teaches PSHE with attention to sex and health education and drug misuse;
- utilises links with the community that can contribute to learning;
- builds constructive links with other institutions.

The principles of 'Best Value', although applicable to just about every aspect of the Evaluation Schedule, can quite easily be applied to this section, especially the principle of 'challenge'.

In primary schools, the quality of curricular and other opportunities offered to pupils at your school could be considered 'very good or excellent' if:

The curriculum interprets statutory requirements in stimulating as well as structured ways, providing for high achievement, particularly in core subjects, and offering pupils a wealth of additional opportunities. It uses resources from within and outside the school very effectively to enrich the curriculum. High priority is given to developing pupils' facility in the basic skills across subjects.

ABOUT

THE PRINCIPLES OF 'BEST VALUE'

The framework for 'best value' is closely linked to the Evaluation Schedule. It comprises the four 'Cs':

1 Compare

2 Challenge

3 Consult

4 Compete

These four Cs form the basis of what a school *can* but is not *required* to ask itself about its performance. In *The Handbooks for Inspecting Schools* [9], inspectors are encouraged to find out the extent to which schools ask and answer questions such as:

Compare:

● What is the quality of education provided by similar schools?

● How do our standards compare with theirs?

● Are we a relatively high performer?

● Do we cost more or less than others?

● Why?

Challenge:

● Why are we doing this?

● Is it what people want?

● What is the evidence about level of need?

● Could someone else do it differently or better?

Consult:

Finding out from staff, pupils, parents and others:

● What they want the school to do;

● What they think of proposed changes or major expenditure;

● Whether they are happy with, or at, the school;

● What is in their best interests.

continued over

ABOUT

THE PRINCIPLES OF 'BEST VALUE' *continued*

Compete:

- Are we providing the service at the right price?
- Could we or others provide the service at a better price?
- What do the users of this service want?
- What is in the best interests of pupils and parents?
- How does the school ensure that it receives the most economic, efficient and effective service from those who provide services to pupils and staff?

The aim is that an Ofsted inspection provides the means for interested local people to reach their own conclusions as to whether best value is being positively achieved. So, while it is not essential that schools assess themselves against these principles, to do so is very much in their interests.

As an individual teacher, it is worth thinking about best value and what your personal impact on it can be. Such an exercise usually highlights how extensively the success of a school is dependent on the effectiveness of the entire school's staff working as a team.

Pupils' personal development is promoted through opportunities for pupils to take significant responsibility and initiative. Pupils clearly understand what is right and wrong, and show a high degree of respect for the differences between people and for their values and beliefs. The curriculum draws positively on the pupils' own cultural, family and religious backgrounds.

'Satisfactory and better' are described as follows:
The curriculum meets the statutory requirements, including those for children aged five and under, and takes account of the National Strategies for literacy and numeracy. Some additional activities are provided which are suitable for children of different ages and needs.

Reasonable use is made of resources within the community; visits
and other activities are planned to contribute to pupils' learning.
Some opportunities for responsibility and initiative are provided.
Pupils understand the difference between right and wrong, and
respect the traditions, values and beliefs of others.

In secondary schools, curricular and other opportunities offered
to pupils at your school could be 'very good or excellent' if:

The curriculum interprets statutory requirements, including the
required elements within the National Curriculum subjects, in a
stimulating way, encouraging high achievement, and provides for
religious education in accordance with an agreed syllabus.
Depending on the needs of students, there is also work-related
provision of high quality. It uses resources from within and outside
the school very effectively to enrich the curriculum. High priority is
given to pupils' personal development through opportunities for
pupils to take responsibility and initiative, and to become aware of
their part in the school and wider community. Pupils debate and
reflect on social and moral issues, appreciate what is right and
wrong, and respect the differences and similarities between people,
their values and beliefs, drawing on pupils' own cultural, religious
and family beliefs.

'Satisfactory or better' will apply to secondary schools where:

The curriculum meets the statutory requirements and offers work-
related courses as appropriate. Reasonable use is made of resources
within the community; visits and other activities are planned to
contribute to pupils' learning. Some opportunities for responsibility
and initiative are provided. Most pupils understand the differences
between right and wrong, and respect the traditions, values and
beliefs of others.

In both primary and secondary schools, this section of the Evaluation Schedule cannot be considered to be satisfactory if:

ABOUT

THE SPIRITUAL, MORAL, SOCIAL AND CULTURAL DEVELOPMENT OF PUPILS

▶ This is an important aspect of any inspection about which much has been written. There are inherent difficulties for anyone having to make judgements on these aspects of pupil development, not least because such an assessment must necessarily be limited by the spiritual, moral, social and cultural (SMSC) development of the assessors, and professional perspectives naturally differ. There remains little consensus of opinion on what constitutes, for example, 'spiritual development'.

▶ SMSC development must (and usually does) underpin all education to varying degrees. It must also be capable of engaging pupils on many levels, particularly cognitively, experientially and emotionally. Yet it can be difficult, when seeking to review exactly how pupils can develop in this way, to ascertain what is meant by spiritual, social, moral and cultural (especially 'spiritual'), and whether or not they can in fact be measured. Personal growth is an enormously complex notion that does not sit happily in any one area of the curriculum. Rather, every aspect of a school's curriculum can take responsibility for SMSC development.

▶ This book cannot afford the space to do justice to this vitally important aspect of school life. SMSC development carries high educational ideals. For the purposes of inspection, it may be easier for classroom teachers to consider the SMSC development of their pupils under the section of the Evaluation Schedule that focuses on how well pupils are taught (section 3), rather than as a separate entity. This approach should make the interconnectedness of SMSC development and other kinds of pupil development (such as academic) easier to see.

▶ *Pastoral Care in Education* (Volume 7, No. 1, March 1999) carries an interesting article on education and spirituality.

- *Statutory requirements, including any significant aspects of the core subjects, are not met and/or;*
- *Opportunities for promoting essential skills are neglected (secondary);*
- *Little or no account is taken of the National Strategies for literacy and numeracy, especially where standards of literacy and numeracy are not high enough (primary);*
- *Little is done to inculcate respect, tolerance and good behaviour;*
- *It is unduly narrow in opportunities for personal development or curricular enrichment (or work-related learning in secondary schools).*

Curricular enrichment is usually achieved through extra-curricular activities. Some schools go as far as offering organised compulsory enrichment programmes so that pupils can develop further in directions of their choosing. For the classroom teacher, enrichment usually means providing some sort of non-compulsory subject or hobby-related club or a study/homework skills group. Enrichment can also be achieved through museum/theatre visits, or work with or in the community; the ideas are endless. If any such activities are offered at your school, inspectors will want to ensure that they are 'socially inclusive' or open to all.

Clearly, for a good deal of this section of the Evaluation Schedule, your school's overall ethos will dictate to a certain degree how successful it can be. In terms of preparing pupils for the next stages of their lives (perhaps the move to secondary school, college or the workplace), your school will have to show that it can provide consistent support and advice, and that pupils are competent in their literacy and numeracy skills across the curriculum.

How well does the school care for its pupils?

Inspectors will need to scrutinise these three main areas under this section of the Evaluation Schedule:

1 How your school ensures the welfare, health and safety of its pupils, and what its arrangements are for child protection.

2 How effective your school is at monitoring its pupils' academic performance, personal development and attendance.

3 How effective your school is at offering support (be it educational or personal) to raise achievements.

The rationale underlying this aspect of the Evaluation Schedule is that, without adequate care, pupils will not be in a position to learn and absorb what is presented to them. Your school will want to show that all members of the pupil community are cared for, in particular any vulnerable individuals. This means that *knowing* every pupil is essential for all schools and indeed all teachers.

In primary and secondary schools, these characteristics can be attributed if they are 'very good or better' at caring for pupils:

Teachers know individual pupils very well, including those from particular groups or those with SEN, and are fully aware of their physical, emotional and intellectual needs. They respond to them in a positive and supportive way. The day-to-day working of the school, in terms of supervision, awareness of hazards within and beyond the school, and the promotion of healthy living, creates a strong sense of the importance of health and safety of pupils. The school has effective practices to identify how well pupils are making progress, particularly in the core subjects, and the achievements of different groups. This identification is followed by good diagnosis of what such groups do well and how they might improve. The school has effective ways of being aware of developing patterns in pupils' behaviour or attendance and relating these patterns to achievement. The systematic monitoring of pupils leads to changes or modifications to the curriculum, for example, or to individual support for pupils' performance and development.

The care a primary or secondary school has for its pupils will be 'satisfactory or better' if:

Teachers know pupils well, recognise their needs and respond well to them. The working environment is safe and pupils are well supervised at work and at play. The school maintains records of pupils' achievements in most aspects of the core curriculum, and individual action plans are in place and used for pupils with special educational needs to monitor progress and guide teaching. The school promotes good behaviour and attendance through agreed, shared and successfully implemented policies. The monitoring of pupils' performance and development that the school carries out is used to make changes in approach and emphasis.

The care that a school shows its pupils will not be satisfactory if:

● It does not take reasonable steps to ensure the care of individual pupils and minimise the possibility of significant harm;

● It does not have satisfactory arrangements to track the progress of pupils in English and mathematics (primary) or across the subjects and courses they study (secondary), and take action to raise achievement;

● It does not adequately monitor and deal with problems of behaviour and attendance.'

The welfare and safety of pupils is thought to be closely linked to the care that pupils receive. Schools and teachers may at least want to show that:

- each pupil has at least one teacher that knows him or her well (for example, a form tutor or class teacher), and that teacher is in a position to liaise with other key members of staff;
- pupils and staff have a safe environment in which to work;
- harassment and bullying are actively discouraged in the promotion of good behaviour.

There are strong links here with the part of the Evaluation Schedule that deals with how well pupils are taught.

It is important for teachers to realise that they may be questioned in detail about the individual needs of pupils and what strategies they adopt to help pupils. Inspectors are actually asked to ensure that teachers are *'consistent and convincing'* in their responses to such questions.

Consistency will also be looked for in the way in which staff reward pupils for good behaviour and sanction them for poor behaviour.

Naturally, assessment makes a feature in this section of the Evaluation Schedule, and inspectors will be looking to see whether assessment is an integral part of teaching and learning at the school. Where appropriate, inspectors will search for evidence of co-operation throughout the school to ensure consistency.

How well does the school work in partnership with parents?

In order to assess this, inspectors will need to take account of:

- The views of your pupils, parents and carers.
- How effective the links your school has with parents and carers are.
- How the involvement of parents and carers impacts the work of your school.

By taking these factors into account, inspectors will aim to determine the level of satisfaction that parents and carers have for your school, the quality of information given to parents and carers about the school, and how well your school's links with parents and carers impact pupils' learning both at home and at school.

Inspectors will use the parents' questionnaire to help them reach decisions on these factors, and are advised to use their *'professional judgement'* on the number of responses on a particular issue that constitutes a strength or a weakness in the eyes of parents and carers.

They will also use their meeting with parents to explore further any issues that arise from the questionnaire.

Do be aware that parents are entitled to request to speak to inspectors during an inspection, and that inspectors will almost certainly want to talk to any parents that help out at your school, such as parent governors or members of the parents' association. Inspectors will also want to ascertain how well parents and staff can talk informally together, and how effectively your school follows up any information passed from parents. With the 'best value' framework in mind, inspectors will be assessing the skills of your school at the principle of consultation.

Primary schools could have these characteristics if their work in partnership with parents and carers is judged to be 'very good or excellent':

The school has a very good range of productive and consistent links with parents and carers that help pupils learn. These extend, for example, from involvement in hearing individual children read, to homework projects and workshops. The mechanisms for exchanging information between school and home work well and include opportunities for parents and carers to give information to the school about their child. Information to parents and carers through written reports is excellent, making clear what pupils need to do to improve and how parents can help. There is strong parental satisfaction with the school, based on secure understanding and regular involvement in its work. There is evidence of improvement in children's learning, behaviour and personal development resulting from good liaison with parents and carers.

Primary schools working in a 'satisfactory or better' way with parents and carers will have these characteristics:

The school has effective links with parents and carers to consolidate and extend pupils' learning. Parents are, in the main, satisfied with the standards achieved and what the school provides, with no major concerns. Reports to parents are clear and useful, and the exchange of information is sound.

Secondary schools could have these characteristics if their work in partnership with parents and carers is judged to be 'very good or excellent':

The school has a very good range of productive and consistent links with parents that help pupils learn. The mechanisms for exchanging information between school and home are effective and include opportunities for parents to give information to the school about their son or daughter. Information to parents through written reports is of good quality, making clear what pupils need to do to improve and what parents can do to help. There is strong parental satisfaction within the school, based on secure understanding and regular involvement in its work. There should be clear improvement in pupils' learning, behaviour and personal development resulting from good liaison with parents.

Secondary schools working in a 'satisfactory or better' way with parents and carers could have these characteristics:

The school has effective links with parents to support pupils' learning. Parents are, in the main, satisfied with the standards achieved and what the school provides, with no major concerns. Reports to parents are clear and useful, and the exchange of information is sound.

Inspectors will not be able to assess your school's partnership with parents as being satisfactory or above if:

- *There is a significant degree of dissatisfaction among parents about the school's work, which is supported by inspection findings;*
- *Information to parents does not give a clear view of pupils' progress (secondary), particularly in English and Mathematics (primary);*
- *Parents are kept at arm's length and the school makes little effort to communicate with them and involve them in the life of the school.'*

How well is the school led and managed?

This is a complex area of the Evaluation Schedule, requiring inspectors to consider, evaluate and report on many aspects of your school's management. Perhaps it is not of direct relevance to classroom teachers, but it is important to know how those who lead you will be judged in their performance, and you may well be questioned by inspectors who are aiming to determine the quality of leadership and management in your school. For example, inspectors will have to consider:

1 The efficiency and effectiveness with which your school is led and managed (with emphasis on the promotion of high standards of teaching and learning).

2 The work of the governing body and whether it fulfils its statutory responsibilities.

3 The effectiveness of your school's systems of performance evaluation – in other words, how it identifies strengths and weaknesses and how improvements are harnessed.

4 The way that your school uses resources (in particular financial), how closely spending is linked to educational priorities, and how the 'best value' principles are applied in your school's use of resources.

5 Staffing, accommodation and learning resources at your school and how they impact educational achievements.

This means that, in order to reach such conclusions, inspectors will want to consider:
- how well your managers direct your school while promoting high standards;
- how great the commitment to your schools' aims and values is;
- how closely teaching is evaluated, monitored and further developed;
- how effective are the systems for appraisal and performance management;
- how well your school sets priorities and targets, and works towards them;
- the shared commitment to improvement held by the management and staff;

- how well governors understand the strengths and weaknesses of the school, as well as how efficiently they assist in shaping the direction of the school;
- how effective is delegation in the management team;
- the extent to which ICT is used effectively by your school's management;
- how well the numbers and qualifications of staff fit the demands of the curriculum;
- whether your school's accommodation and learning resources allow for the curriculum to be taught effectively to the full range of pupils at your school;
- (of particular interest to NQTs) whether the induction for new members of staff is effective, and whether your school could provide effective initial teacher training;
- how well the principles of 'best value' are applied in the management of your school and its resources.

In order to achieve this extensive evaluation of your school's management, inspectors are advised to focus on the impact that management has on your school as a whole, including standards achieved and general ethos, as well as the processes of management. This means that the impact of your school's management will be under scrutiny, rather than simply *how* your school is managed. Performance management in your school will also be a focus. In short, inspectors will want to see that a commitment to high standards and improvement is evident.

In both primary and secondary schools, these characteristics can be applied where the management of a school is 'very good or better':

The leaders of the school share a common purpose and put pupils and their achievements first. They build co-operative and co-ordinated teams and use assessment evidence well, to set high goals for pupils and challenging targets for the school and for individual staff. Staff in the school reflect critically on what they can do to improve learning and develop more effective ways of working. The work of the school is fully and thoroughly monitored, particularly the quality of teaching and its impact, and the behaviour of pupils. There is good delegation to staff with management responsibilities and effective follow-up to ensure that tasks are completed well. Governors monitor performance and have a good understanding of the strengths and weaknesses of the school and the challenges it faces, and set the right priorities for development and improvement. They fulfil their statutory duties well in providing a sense of direction for the school. They understand and apply best value principles.

In both primary and secondary schools, these characteristics can be applied where the management of a school is 'satisfactory or better':

The leadership and management of the school are clear about its strengths and weaknesses, and have established some ways of securing improvement in the average level of standards achieved. Teamwork is mostly well established and the school has identified the right tasks for the future. Most staff share a common purpose and have taken steps to make their work more effective. Staff with particular responsibilities are clear about what these are and how they will measure their success. Governors have a sound sense of the strengths and weaknesses of the school and are working with staff in their efforts to improve. They meet their statutory responsibilities.

The leadership and management at your school, whether primary or secondary, are unlikely to be satisfactory if:

- teaching at your school is unsatisfactory in a significant number of cases;
- staff show significant complacency;
- standards could be significantly higher;
- the senior management team, including the governors, do not know the strengths and weaknesses of the school.

Inspectors will have at their disposal an enormous amount of information in order to make these judgements about your school's leadership and management. In addition to their interviews with staff and general observations, they will be able to refer to the paperwork that will have been prepared for them by your managers.

In short, inspectors will be looking for evidence of a clear vision for your school, in which there is the space and inclination for the management of change and the ongoing development of a highly performing team. A sense of inspiration and motivation may well pervade in such a school, with effective leaders presenting sound examples for staff. They will also need to establish whether or not the leadership and management at your school enables middle managers, such as heads of year or department, to perform their responsibilities effectively.

The skills of communication that your leaders and managers have will form the focus of scrutiny, in particular how well they bring staff together in a mutual understanding of what your school needs to do in order to improve and the priorities that should be applied. This could form the basis of questions that you may be asked by inspectors. You may also be asked about how interested you feel your managers are in the work that you do.

Of particular interest to most teachers will be the paragraph in *The Handbooks for Inspecting Schools* that states:

> *One indication of the competence and confidence of the headteacher is the way the run-up to the inspection has been managed. Has the headteacher taken it in his or her stride, not allowing it to be too much of a distraction to staff and to the school's work and purpose, or has the inspection prompted unnecessary work and been allowed to induce unnecessary stress? Is on-site inspection managed well by the school?*

As far as overseeing the performance of individual teachers, inspectors will be looking to see whether teachers are given any assistance in analysing how best to work with particular groups. This may not necessarily come from managers themselves, but may come from other teachers with particular strengths.

This is a detailed part of the Evaluation Schedule, covering many aspects of school life. What have been presented here are the main points of interest to most teachers. If you would like to know more, please refer to the full guidance in *The Handbooks for Inspecting Schools*[10].

What should the school do to improve further?

When going through this section of the Evaluation Schedule, inspectors will want to identify what your school should include in the action plan that will be drawn up after the inspection. These issues will be related to raising standards, the quality of education that your school offers, and the quality of teaching that exists within your school. It could well be that the issues highlighted here by inspectors as being in need of development will already have been identified by your school in its development plan. If this is the case, the final inspection report should make this clear.

ABOUT

THE SCOPE OF INSPECTIONS

❯ Although inspections reach far and deep into the workings of a school and the functioning of its staff, in particular of its teachers and managers, they do not, in most cases, serve to dictate how you should teach individual classes. Nor, in most cases, do they seek to control the way in which the National Curriculum is delivered. They are an assessment of how well a school is doing, covering strengths and weaknesses (or areas for development), and what may be done to make improvements. In this respect, inspections are important but should not be considered *exceptional* experiences.

❯ It is not helpful to try to equate the judgements made by Ofsted with those that you may make on a child's performance – assessment criteria and methods will undoubtedly be too different to enable useful conclusions to be drawn.

This section of the Evaluation Schedule will also seek to identify other factors that your school should consider for improvement, which will not be included in the issues for action.

Inspectors are advised that they should '*set out what needs to be done to bring about improvement*', but should not '*go further than this to indicate how the school could take the required action*', as that is '*the remit of the school's governors and staff*' [11]. Any issues for action must be closely linked by inspectors to inspection judgements. Inspectors are also advised that the issues identified for further development must be '*big issues*' for your school.

---

1 The Stationery Office publishes the *Handbook for Inspecting Primary and Nursery Schools*, the *Handbook for Inspecting Secondary Schools* and the *Handbook for Inspecting Special Schools and Pupil Referral Units*. They are for use by inspectors.

2 *Handbooks for Inspecting Schools*, published by TSO, 1999.

3 *Handbooks for Inspecting Schools*, TSO, 1999.

4 *Handbook for Inspecting Schools*, TSO, 1999.

5 TSO, 1999.

6 TSO, 1999.

7 *Handbooks for Inspecting Schools*, TSO, 1999.

8 TSO, 1999.

9 TSO, 1999.

10 TSO, 1999.

11 *Handbooks for Inspecting Schools*, TSO, 1999.

CHAPTER 4

The inspection experience

'If we all did the things we're capable of doing, we would literally astound ourselves.' THOMAS EDISON

For most teachers and their schools, inspection does not begin when the team arrives on the first day. There are three distinct stages to inspection, each carrying its own set of challenges and demands.

Before the inspection

This is the first, and potentially most stressful, stage. The period between notice being given of inspection and the event itself can make or break a teacher's view of the entire process and, in extreme cases, of the teaching profession as a whole. For some teachers, this is a sad part of the experience of being inspected. It is therefore hoped that the following section will remove some of the perceived mystery and potential anxiety of the pre-inspection weeks.

Notice of inspection

The amount of notice that your school will be given before an inspection is one of the main areas of change in the current framework for the inspection of schools. The notice of inspection must now be between six and ten school weeks. This period has been reduced so that schools can better avoid the frenzy of document writing and re-writing and any other preparations that your school may feel it should make before the inspectors arrive.

While this change has been heralded as positive by most involved, there is now added pressure on headteachers to complete the necessary documentation on time, and the need for expert efficiency on the part of contractors and registered inspectors is even more heightened.

The inspection of your school will take place during a five-week 'inspection window'. The following steps outline the stages of the notice period:

1 Six school weeks before the inspection window (which is typically eight weeks before the inspection begins), your headteacher will receive notification of inspection. This notification will explain whether the inspection is to be short or full, and will include a full set of inspection forms and a copy of the PICSI report.

2 Five school weeks before the inspection window (around seven weeks before the start of the inspection) your school will return the first form (S1) to Ofsted. The S1 form allows your headteacher and governors to provide basic information about your school. It enables Ofsted to draw up a specification that can be issued to the contractor. Soon afterwards, the contractor who will be running your inspection will receive this specification and a copy of the PICSI report which will assist in the composing of an inspection team. A date will then be set for the inspection, and your school will be informed who the registered inspector is to be. The registered inspector will then contact your school.

3 Two school weeks before the inspection window (usually four weeks before the start of the inspection), the contractor responsible for your school's inspection will send an inspection plan to Ofsted.

4 Four weeks before the inspection your school will send the rest of the pre-inspection forms (S2–S4), previous inspection report, prospectus and development plan to the registered inspector. At this stage, your school will call a meeting for parents, concerning the inspection. Meanwhile, your registered inspector will be analysing and digesting the information sent by your school and will be preparing for a visit.

5 Two or three weeks before the inspection is due to begin, your registered inspector will visit your school. The inspection will then be planned in detail.

6 Two weeks before the inspection, your registered inspector will meet the parents and carers of your school's pupils. S/he can then complete the Pre-Inspection Commentary.

7 Some time before the inspection begins the registered inspector will meet and brief the full inspection team.

ABOUT

INSPECTION 'TEAMS'

❯ A team of inspectors will be inspecting your school, but they will not necessarily have worked together before. It is up to your registered inspector to set the tone for the team and to maximise the use of the skills of individual team inspectors.

❯ Your registered inspector must also ensure that every inspector on his/her team is in a position to perform his/her duties thoroughly and effectively, and that the team works with cohesiveness.

❯ Do not assume that, because the people inspecting your school are called a 'team', they have worked together before, as this may not be the case. Indeed, it has been known for some teams only to meet for the first time just prior to the start of the inspection; however, this is far from ideal and Ofsted makes it clear that it is not acceptable.

When your registered inspector makes contact with your head-teacher, s/he will be wanting to establish how the forthcoming inspection is being viewed by your school. Excessive anxiety may be an indicator that there is an issue in your school that the inspectors should focus on. In addition to this, Ofsted has often been keen to point out that the success of an inspection can be dependent on the willingness of the school to work with inspectors and actively demonstrate what has been achieved. Your registered inspector will also discuss and agree times and dates for the other pre-inspection events, such as meeting staff and parents, and will make the *Curriculum Vitae* of every member of the inspection team available to the school.

EXAMPLE: When the forms S1–S4 arrived, I had not previously appreciated how long it would take me to complete them. I really had to rely on other staff members to allow me uninterrupted space to get through them. It worked fairly well; colleagues fielded situations that I would normally be involved in, and between us we created space for me to focus on this important stage.

My advice to teachers in other schools would be to use other sources of advice and support while these forms are being completed, and for other heads to ensure that there is someone available to cover temporarily for them during this time. I found that communicating these stages to all staff, and explaining why I would perhaps be a little less accessible for a short time, helped us through this step.

When changes to the schedule are made

It is important to be aware that, even though the contractors, Ofsted, your registered inspector and your headteacher may have fixed a date for the inspection of your school, this date is not necessarily set in stone and may be subject to change. Likewise, the inspection team itself may change, and a change in inspection personnel may mean that it is necessary to change the originally agreed date.

Such alterations to what is expected at the pre-inspection stage can be extremely unsettling and even stressful. Your headteacher should keep staff informed of each development, which will help you to take any last-minute changes in your stride. Although easier said than done, do try to retain that all-important perspective. Last-minute changes, while annoying and potentially disappointing, do not have to signal crises.

Pre-inspection stages for your school

Once the necessary forms have been completed and returned to the relevant bodies, there are clear stages for a school to go through in the lead-up to an inspection. While preparation may vary from school to school, depending on how the senior management teams handle the imminent event, at the very least the following will happen:

The registered inspector will visit your school. The purpose of this visit, according to the *Handbooks for Inspecting Schools*[1], is:

a *To establish a good and trusting working relationship between (the registered inspector) and the school, particularly the headteacher;*

b *To gain a better understanding of the school, its nature, what it is aiming to do and how it goes about its work;*

c *To consider aspects of the school on which inspectors might focus, some of which may be identified by the school;*

d *To brief the staff and any governors who are able to meet you on how the inspection will work;*

e *To agree the necessary arrangements for the inspection.'*

Many headteachers now aim to ensure that staff meet the registered inspector as soon as possible, and that *all* staff members are in a position to meet him/her. This should be a priority for staff members too – try not to let anything stand in the way of your being able to meet (and talk to, if possible) this all-important player in the inspection process.

Registered inspectors are expected to answer any queries that staff may have at this stage, so do not let the opportunity pass if you have something you would like to ask. Some headteachers gather questions and concerns from staff in advance, so that they can be sure they will be dealt with in good time. If this arrangement has been set up at your school, take advantage if necessary. Above all, do not let this meeting come and go without having your concerns allayed and questions answered. This is a very busy time for the registered inspector, but s/he cannot be too busy to communicate with teachers. If this is the case, consider the option of making a complaint (see pages 89–93).

Registered inspectors are told that '*your meetings with the headteacher, staff and governors should put them at their ease by explaining how the inspection team will be run, and give them confidence in the process. They should be helped to see how they can gain value from it*' [2]. Staff concerns and anxieties should be passed on to inspection team members by the registered inspector at the team briefing before the inspection begins. This is why it is vitally important for your headteacher to communicate what these may be, and whether or not staff members collectively are facing any particularly adverse circumstances that may be having an effect on individuals, such as the death or serious illness of a colleague, pupil or family member.

While inspectors are visiting your school, they will need a base from which to work. If there is suitable accommodation allocated to them, this may need to be prepared in advance. However, the provision of a space for inspectors to use should not interrupt the work of your school, nor should it inconvenience any teacher; so do not fear that you will lose your staffroom or, even worse, your office/work room or classroom. It is not acceptable for any teacher to be removed from his or her usual working space in order to accommodate visiting inspectors. Indeed, inspectors are told that they must make their own arrangements if no suitable room can be found within your school. If this happens to you and it causes undue stress or inconvenience, you have grounds to raise the issue with your headteacher and expect a resolution.

The pre-inspection meeting between parents and the registered inspector is a legal requirement. This meeting must take place before the inspection begins (usually around two weeks before). The views of your pupils' parents and carers are considered to be important pre-inspection evidence and your school's 'appropriate body' (usually the governing body) will be expected to ensure that parents have every opportunity to attend. Staff are not invited to this meeting unless they are the parent or carer of a child at the school. Ofsted has suggested to registered inspectors that the following topics should be discussed:

- the standards your school achieves;
- how your school helps pupils, whatever their ability, to learn and make progress;
- the attitudes and values your school promotes;
- behaviour and attendance;
- the work your school expects pupils to do at home, your school's links with parents – including information on how pupils are getting on;
- how your school responds to parents' suggestions and concerns;
- how your school has improved in recent years.

A draft letter to parents and agenda for the parents' meeting can be found in Appendices 3 and 4.

Your registered inspector will, at some stage, ask your governing body to distribute the standard questionnaire to parents. This is not a compulsory requirement, and your headteacher and governors may choose not to distribute the questionnaire. That said, it would be unusual in the extreme if your school refused to offer parents this opportunity to contribute their thoughts and feelings. Parents are given questionnaires on the basis of one per pupil, and their responses are strictly confidential (i.e. no one at your school should know what has been written).

Likewise, at the parents' meeting, parents are instructed not to mention individual teachers or pupils by name. If there are particular language needs among your school's parents, the contractor will supply translated forms and your registered inspector may have to arrange for translation of any responses received in a foreign language. This way, all parents should be offered equal opportunities to contribute their views. It seems to be a common experience for schools that when inspectors begin to probe, parents get firmly behind the school with fierce loyalty. For this reason, the parents' meeting is often very positively in favour of the school.

As soon as possible after the parents' meeting, the registered inspector will analyse the questionnaires and look for possible issues that may need to become a focus for the inspection. Significant issues should be discussed with your headteacher at this stage, and s/he will be given the opportunity to present other evidence of the views that your school's parents have. The opinions of parents form part of the final written report.

Documentary 'evidence' required

Your inspectors will need a selection of 'evidence' of the work of your school in order to make the judgements they must make. Apart from forms S1–S4, PICSI report, the last inspection report, the current school development plan and your school's prospectus, inspectors may also require:

1 A copy of your school's timetable/programme.

2 A staff handbook (if your school has one) or a list of staff responsibilities/objectives.

3 A plan of the school.

4 The governors' annual report to parents.

5 Minutes of the meetings of the governing body.

6 Evidence of progress towards the targets set by governors.

7 The outcomes of recent self-evaluations carried out by the school.

8 The outcomes of any external monitoring and evaluations carried out since the last inspection.

9 Samples of pupils' earlier and current work. The exact nature of this sample will be decided between your registered inspector (although two above average, two average and two below average in each year group/subject is the norm apart from in very small schools). This sample may not be made available to inspectors before the first day of the inspection. In short inspections, it is restricted to English and Mathematics (primary) and end of key stage work in the core subjects (secondary). The achievements of statemented children in both secondary and primary schools are also analysed. In full inspections, the work of pupils in all year groups and subjects as well as that of statemented pupils will be analysed.

10 Any other documentation your headteacher and governors wish the inspectors to consider (subject to their agreement).

During the actual inspection, your inspectors will also be able to access schemes of work, planning and assessment documents, attendance registers, pupil's records and reports, any documents relating to pupils with special educational needs and the daily lesson planning of teachers. However, Ofsted does view school policy documents as a matter of self-audit for your school and they should only be called on if a concern should arise about the implementation of a policy in a particular area.

In short inspections, the documentary evidence required is considerably less and in most cases, is not removed from the school.

Regardless of whether your school is facing a short or a long inspection, Ofsted is adamant that '*No one should develop or rework documents especially for the inspection. Wherever practicable, inspectors will accept data in the form held by schools.*'[3] Only if it will not cause you undue stress and pressure should you contemplate reworking anything.

If you are directed to develop or rework any policies or documents, speak to your union rep if adequate non-contact time is not granted. It is most important that your workload does not increase dramatically before an inspection and your managers and leaders should be working hard to ensure this is so. Besides, preparing copious amounts of literature for inspectors will surely put them off the scent of your fabulous teaching, so resist the temptation! As long as all documents and policies are subject to annual appraisal or updating, and you are aware of the extent of your responsibilities to this end, inspectors will be happy. They know that, in the most effective schools, policies can never *all* be up to date.

Preparation of the registered inspector

Throughout the pre-inspection stages for your school, it is not just teachers who will be preparing. In the weeks before the inspection begins your registered inspector should be:

- Ensuring that there is a team member to cover all subjects, special educational needs and equal opportunities;
- Working out how the team can best be deployed, taking the expertise of individuals into consideration;
- Devising a schedule at least for the first day of inspection;
- Planning the collection of evidence that relates to the inspection focal points in the *pre-inspection commentary* (the 'big picture' of your school);
- Planning with your school when feedback to subject co-ordinators and classroom teachers will take place;
- Setting deadlines for inspectors by which draft sections for the final report must be completed.

The registered inspector will also need to complete the *Pre-inspection Commentary* (see page 15). In this commentary, s/he will be presenting hypotheses as to why standards at your school are as they are and will also hypothesise on whether or not your school might be underachieving, have serious weaknesses, or even require special measures (see page 193).

Before the actual inspection begins, the registered inspector will need to arrange to meet the rest of his or her team for a team briefing, which must be held at a time that does not encroach on inspection time. Inspectors *must* attend this meeting because this is when they will find out about:

- the contents of the pre-inspection commentary;
- any concerns and anxieties that staff members may have about the inspection;
- their first day's programme of inspection;
- organisation and administration for the inspection.

The registered inspector will also use this opportunity to remind inspectors to ensure that they collect evidence against every heading in the Evaluation Schedule, and also to make sure that they abide by the Code of Conduct that is expected of them.

ABOUT

BECOMING FAMILIAR WITH THE INSPECTION DOCUMENTATION

> Preparation for an inspection should certainly not involve inordinate amounts of additional work for anyone in your school's community. If it does, it can hardly be called a true and proper appraisal of the work of the inspected! However, one area in which it is well worth investing a little time and attention is in becoming familiar with the inspection documentation. The fact that you are reading this book (which has included the most important aspects of this literature) is a great start, but if you want to read about inspection straight from 'the horse's mouth', take a look at the documents listed below. This does not mean reading them all cover to cover, but it will certainly ease any pre-inspection anxiety you may be feeling if you get to know exactly what it is that will (or at least should) be happening.

> *The Handbooks for Inspecting Schools* (available for primary, secondary and special schools and pupil referral units), published by The Stationery Office (TSO), 1999. These are available from the TSO website: **www.tso-online.co.uk**, or from good bookshops.

> *Inspecting Schools: The Framework*, published by Ofsted, effective from January 2000. Available from the Ofsted publications centre on 0207 510 0180, or the website: **www.ofsted.gov.uk**.

> *Making the Most of Inspection*, published by Ofsted, fully revised version, 1998. Available from the Ofsted publications centre on 0207 510 0180, or the website: **www.ofsted.gov.uk**

> Ofsted is keen to point out to teachers that staff and governors will get far more out of the inspection process as 'active participants' rather than 'passive recipients'. This is one way of encouraging activity over passivity. Also, it has been said before but is worth stressing again, that there are differences between inspection teams in the way they carry out inspections. Knowing what should and should not happen gives you a fine layer of protection should you need it.

During the inspection

When the inspectors actually arrive in your school, a new set of challenges present themselves. If your preparation has been balanced, this should be a relatively stress-free and even enjoyable time.

Obligations of your inspectors

In order to be in a position to write a report on your school, inspectors must spend a substantial amount of their time during inspection (at least 60 per cent) observing lessons, sampling pupils' work and teachers' records, and talking to pupils. They will also want to observe assemblies, extra-curricular activities, registration and tutorial periods, and hold discussions with pupils, staff (especially those with management responsibilities) and governors.

During the time that inspectors are visiting your school, they must also offer verbal feedback on the evidence they have gathered. Throughout the duration of the inspection, your inspectors must abide by the standards that are expected of them, including the Code of Conduct (page 5) and the Quality Guarantee (page 4).

If your experience of inspection is that your inspectors are not adhering to this Code of Conduct and Quality Guarantee, it is very important to raise your concerns with your headteacher. Be sure to keep a written record of the issues that you raise and your evidence for doing so.

Teacher/inspector relationship

'It is illogical to expect smiles from others if one does not smile oneself. Therefore, one can see that many things depend on one's own behaviour.' HIS HOLINESS THE DALAI LAMA

'The snow goose need not bathe to make itself white. Neither need you do anything but be yourself.' LAO-TZU

Building a good relationship with your inspector(s) once they arrive at your school is of paramount importance. It is not enough to assume that *you* should respond to *them*; an inspection should never be done *to* you. The relationship must be open to growth from both 'sides', which means that your input into what will make it work best for you is as valid as the inspector's input into what will make it work best for him or her.

Taking the time to build a rapport with inspectors, put across your character and take ownership of what happens will help you to influence (if not manage) your inspection. It would not be appropriate to act in a deferential manner towards inspectors. If anything, think of them as professional equals contributing to the delivery of the education service in this country, as indeed are all your teaching colleagues.

When thinking about your relationship with your inspector(s), these ideas may help:

1 Do not assume anything negative about the relationship before it has had time to develop. Be optimistic about its potential.

2 Be aware of the fact that, for many teachers, their professional life draws heavily on the essence of all that is them – their very character and personality. Their style and performance is *them*. If this may be the case for you, consider how this could cloud your relationship with inspectors if you feel judged as you *the person*, rather than you *the teacher*.

3 A great deal hangs on the skills of inspectors in making teachers feel at ease throughout the inspection process, but do not absolve yourself of all responsibility here! It is the combination of what teachers and inspectors bring to such relationships that determine its success.

4 Trust is central to the inspector/teacher relationship. However, you may be limiting your relationship if you insist on waiting for inspectors to prove their trustworthiness.

5 There is anecdotal evidence to suggest that the manner of inspectors has a direct impact on the way in which the final inspection report is received by teachers. In many ways this is a great shame, as the opportunity for development is marginalised by clumsy interactions of character and (on occasion) ego. There is really no antidote to this,

apart from taking the time and effort to develop a relationship in which you can discuss the inspection with mutual understanding and respect. That said, there is no excuse for inhumane inspectors, and if you feel that this has been your experience you should make your feelings known.

6   There is also some anecdotal evidence to suggest that inspectors are generally seen less favourably by classroom teachers than by headteachers. This could be because heads have the opportunity to build deeper relationships with inspectors through ongoing debriefings and discussions. If there is any truth in this, it supports the need to do all in your power to get to know those who are inspecting you.

7   It is possible to find out a considerable amount about those who will be inspecting you. The search engine on the Ofsted website allows you enter the names of inspectors to see what, when and where they have inspected in the past. Combined with the fact that the *Curricula Vitae* of inspectors, which all contractors must supply to the schools that those inspectors will be visiting, a significant amount of information can be obtained. If you decide to investigate your inspectors in this way, do be mindful of the extent to which the conclusions that you reach block the development of good working relationships.

8   Enjoy your guests! This is not a flippant statement – many who do not have the focus of inspection/appraisal find the feedback desert a difficult place to flourish.

The worst scenario in the teacher/inspector relationship is a total breakdown in communication. This is not unknown and is a terribly sad situation. The potential for positive gain from an inspection in which this has happened is negligible, and the stress and anxiety caused to both teachers and inspectors involved is tremendous.

As a teacher and an individual, it is very important to keep lines of communication open for as long as possible, regardless of what might be happening elsewhere in your school. Even if the situation deteriorates beyond repair for your school as a whole, there may still be some positive thread to be gained for you as an individual.

The former Chief Inspector of Schools, Chris Woodhead, described inspection as an act of '*disciplined subjectivity*'. There is a case for good relationships with inspectors, if ever there was one!

> *EXAMPLE: My experience of Ofsted and similar style inspections has been quite mixed; I have encountered both the rudest and also the most understanding inspectors. Consequently, I believe that the degree to which such experiences prove to be positive depends quite heavily on the personalities of those doing the inspection (and especially the team leader). I guess that the type of Ofsted inspector that I really dislike is the one that never smiles, has a very controlling attitude, and does not appear to be listening. In my opinion, s/he is responsible if the system has a bad name amongst a group of teachers.*
>
> *Conversely, I have experienced Ofsted inspectors who are terribly kind and have made efforts to put staff at their ease. One woman that I recall in particular almost went over the top with her politeness and her smiles, but it worked a treat. She also gave very positive feedback and appeared to view me as a source of valuable evidence as much as she did the paperwork and the observation.*

Pupil/inspector relationship

Anyone who has read the autobiographical books of Gervase Phinn [4] will know that pupils can sometimes seem intent on performing their own inspection of the inspectors! Regardless of the direction in which your inspector wants to lead his or her discussions with pupils, the children's agendas can sometimes dominate. There is nothing wrong with this. It is far better for your pupils to feel free to converse with inspectors, than for them to be so struck with terror that they feel unable to utter a word.

ABOUT

COVER LESSONS

> ❯ The dreaded cover lesson is the cause of so much anxiety during inspections, but this really is unnecessary. If you know you will need cover during the inspection week, it would be a good idea to ensure, if at all possible, that the work you set is not only straightforward for a cover teacher (who may well be a non-specialist) to follow, but can show pupil progress too.

> ❯ If you find yourself having to cover for a colleague during the inspection, do not worry about the prospect of being observed. The line from Ofsted is that the observation of cover lessons should not have a significant impact on the final report, unless they are taken by a supply teacher who does a substantial amount of work at the school. Inspectors are well aware that cover lessons are often delivered by non-specialists and that they usually eat into a teachers' non-contact time (in secondary schools).

> ❯ If you feel that you have received harsh treatment over the observation of a cover lesson, make sure that your registered inspector knows your views. Your headteacher will be the person to facilitate this.

When talking to pupils, inspectors will aim to find out what they know, can do and understand, and whether or not they are at or near their limits of learning. They will also want to find out if your pupils have the ability to apply the knowledge that they have in different contexts. Such discussions will ordinarily take place during lessons, but should not intrude into your teaching time.

Outside lessons, inspectors will want to find out from pupils how they view their school and how far their interests are supported. In gathering all this information, inspectors will be looking out in particular for incidental talk and contributions that pupils make in class, including questions initiated by them and their answers to questions posed by you.

Never feel intimidated when you see the inspectors talk to your pupils. Pupils are the ones receiving the education you and your school are offering, and their views should be taken into consideration. If, however, you feel that your pupils' views have been sought more rigorously than your own, discuss the matter with your headteacher who will be able to make sure that your feelings are known by the registered inspector.

ABOUT

OVER-INSPECTION OF AN INDIVIDUAL TEACHER

> Over-inspection of a teacher can occasionally happen. There are several reasons for this, including insufficient liaison between inspectors and the need to observe a certain number of lessons in a school with few teachers. It can also be a problem for those who have had this experience. One very positive way of viewing this is that you would at least know that any judgements made were done so on a substantial amount of evidence.

> However, if over-inspection is taking its toll, do mention to your headteacher what is happening (most heads monitor the amount of observations that their staff experience during an inspection). The headteacher can then raise the matter with your registered inspector who will be able to make sure that you are given some reprieve.

> *The Handbooks for Inspecting Schools* state that teachers should not normally be inspected for more than half of any one day, and never more than three-quarters.

> Under-inspection can be an equally worrying situation. Being kept waiting until near the end of the inspection before being observed can be very unnerving. In theory this should not happen, but oversights do occur. Mention the situation to your headteacher after a couple of days, rather than waiting indefinitely. Your headteacher can then inform your registered inspector who will be able to remedy the situation. It is in your interest to be observed as often as possible, if accurate judgements are to be made on the effectiveness of your teaching.

Not all pupils are enthusiastic about being questioned by individuals they may view as strangers. If a child expresses particular concern about this, you would be perfectly justified in making this known to the inspector in your room. In all cases, inspectors should ensure that any questioning of pupils in lessons is as unobtrusive as possible, and under no circumstances should it disrupt your teaching.

> EXAMPLE: I felt, and still feel, that it is important for pupils to know who is visiting their classroom, especially if that visitor is going to address them individually. I always ask the inspector's name and make a point of introducing him/her to the class.

Other adults in your classroom

While inspectors are at your school, they will almost certainly see the work of all the adults there, and will be particularly interested in the work of those adults who are in a position to have a direct impact on the education offered to pupils. This means that any support teachers, trained non-teaching assistants, SEN assistants and volunteers will need to be briefed on their work with you.

These ideas may help:

● Make sure that any other adults who will be working in your classroom during the inspection week receive copies of relevant lesson plans as early as possible.

● Aim to talk to your helpers in advance of each lesson, to minimise the chances of confusion in front of an inspector. This is not always possible, especially if your helpers also assist other teachers in your school, but it is helpful towards ensuring free-flowing lessons.

● Make sure that your helpers are aware of the possibility of being questioned by inspectors, who will want to seek evidence of the quality of their work. You may want to spend some time together discussing your working relationship and how your partnership adds value to the work in your classroom. Much of this will be implicit in the way you interact, but taking the time to put what you do together into words will ensure that you are both able to maximise the benefits to pupils when questioned by inspectors.

- Encourage support staff (especially those who are unqualified) to enter into a dialogue with inspectors. They do not have to wait until they are spoken to before revealing what a fantastic team you are!

- Show inspectors any written guidance you give to your support staff, especially if you recommend additional readings on topics that might be unfamiliar to them. Also, show them any written methods you may use, to enable your support staff to share information and observations on pupils.

It is unlikely that inspectors will give feedback to individual support staff.

ABOUT

MAKING THE IMPLICIT *EXPLICIT*

- In order to be sure that inspectors get the most accurate picture of your work, you are going to have to *say* as well as *do*. The confidence with which you speak about your work will certainly have an impact on the impression that your inspector forms, so go ahead and be proud. Making the implicit explicit is what it is all about, especially if you act in response to the moment in a way that may not be documented.

- Do not assume that, because some wonderfully positive aspect of your work is mentioned in some of the literature that your inspectors were given, you do not need to talk about it, too. Leave no stone unturned; tell them everything!

Maintaining routine

When the inspectors are in your school, they should endeavour to keep disruption to your usual routines to a minimum. Yet the responsibility for this also lies with your school, so these ideas may help:

- Keep your usual routines going – for example, any clubs you may run or homework support sessions. It is really important that inspectors see the full range of your activities, and that pupils do not get the message that inspection is an exceptional experience.

- Resist the urge to present special impressions during the week of the inspection. Do not rush off at tangents to put together spontaneous clubs or activities!

- It may be wise to postpone any special plans for outings or events that would be better suited to another time. Being off-site undoubtedly puts pressure on remaining teachers, and this could be unnerving during an inspection. It will also help to minimise distractions for pupils.

- If there is a reason why you will not be in school for the full week (perhaps an appointment or some in-service training), it may be wise to rearrange it for another time if possible.

- Maintain your usual pattern of rewards and sanctions. Introducing anything new for the week of the inspection will confuse pupils, and inspectors are sure to spot this!

- If an arranged meeting falls during the inspection week, it would be a good idea to hold it. You may be joined by an inspector or two, but at least you will be showing them some of the 'behind the scenes' work that you are involved in.

Focusing on the positive

During research for this book, many teachers, regardless of their over-all view of being inspected, expressed positive sentiments about the actual week of inspection. Table 4.1 below and opposite is a brief summary.

Table 4.1: Focusing on the positive aspects of inspection

There is something enjoyable about demonstrating what you know and what you can do with skill.

There will be the opportunity and challenge to put right anything that the inspection unearths as needing attention.

Table 4.1 continued

The mind is focused utterly on the task in hand. There is less need to do X while thinking about Y.
Inspection week is an opportunity like no other to think about performance which is often sharper than usual as a result.
You are often much clearer in your mind about how and why you do things.
Receiving good feedback during the course of the week is a major boost.
More open professional dialogues with colleagues are likely, setting a precedent for the future.
Teamwork and team membership is promoted.
Relationships with pupils can flourish further, as you are more likely to spend a little more time on them during the inspection week.
Anecdotal evidence suggests that pupils tend to believe that teachers teach better during inspection time, and teachers tend to believe that pupils are better behaved during inspections.
Talking to inspectors about your work can have therapeutic benefits, offering the chance to gain perspective about what it is that you do; a different sense of your own achievements.
You may spend more time than usual evaluating the work you have done with your class.

EXAMPLE: It wasn't until I was actually talking to an inspector about my work that I realised how negatively I thought of how I worked. Fortunately for me, the inspector took the time to say that she thought I was doing a good job and that I should feel more confident about my abilities. Having presented such a negative view, it was a real boost to be told that, and the impact has lasted way beyond the end of the inspection.

Enjoying the fruits of your preparation

In terms of your day-to-day lesson planning and resource preparation, you have probably never been as prepared as you are during an inspection. Consider these ways of enjoying the fruits of your preparation:

1 You may not have to spend so much time in the evenings working on preparation, because of the time you have previously put in.

2 You will be in a position to talk openly with inspectors about where you are going with your work in the classroom.

3 The potential for staying 'in the moment' during lessons is enhanced, as you may not have to do as much thinking on your feet (if you have this tendency) as usual.

4 Allow yourself time to acknowledge your preparedness. Do not find yet more tasks to do.

5 Now that you have reached this stage of inspection, affirm to yourself that what you have done is at least good enough.

6 Encourage others to enjoy the collective preparation of the school as a whole. Perhaps stay for a drink and chat at the end of the first day.

Your interaction with the inspectors

'For the person who is willing to ask and question, the world will always be new. The skilled questioner and the attentive listener knows how to enter into another's experience.'

MAYKUT AND MOORHOUSE, 1994

Throughout your inspection, those observing your work have a duty to develop a dialogue with you about the work they have seen. This is a great opportunity to further highlight evidence of your success in the classroom and to influence your working relationship with your inspector.

Expect to be asked at least the following:

- why you use particular methods of teaching;
- whether your intentions were met in the lesson you just taught;
- how the lesson fits into the scheme of work.

In many cases, inspectors can offer brief oral feedback at the end of each lesson observed. If the inspector has a concern about your work, feedback may not be so immediate so that the inspector has an opportunity to think about what has been observed. However, do not assume that this is the case if you are not offered immediate feedback; it may just be that your inspector wants to wait for a more mutually convenient time.

As the inspection progresses during the week, your inspector will be in a position to pull together your strengths and weaknesses, having liaised with fellow inspectors who may also have observed your work. You will be given a written record of judgements on your teaching.

When thinking about your interactions with inspectors, these ideas may inspire:

❯ Robin Sieger, author of *Natural Born Winners*[5], has stressed the importance of teachers holding a solid belief in their own abilities when under inspection. He holds that 90 per cent of our communication is non-verbal, so if we *believe* in our professionalism and integrity then our behaviour will be congruent. This has to be worth considering. Indicators of confidence in body language include:

- the ability to maintain eye contact;
- avoiding exaggerated movements;
- keeping a check on nervous fidgeting;
- maintaining a steady voice;
- sitting comfortably in the chair;
- an open stance (nothing crossed);
- smiling.

'Your expressions, in repose, are icons of your attitudes toward life.'
Kare Anderson

❯ Keep dialogues with inspectors going throughout the week of your inspection, so that you are in a position to take corrective measures if you feel that a picture of your work that is not entirely and accurately reflective of what you do is starting to emerge.

❯ Be sure to challenge any statements made about you which you feel do not truly reflect your work. If you can show evidence to the contrary, do so. A sure way to crush your self-esteem is to let unfair statements stand.

➤ Most teachers are aware that it is not through competition with others that bright stars can shine. It is simply about consistent personal and professional standards that are often achieved through collaboration, co-operation and mutual support.

➤ It is extremely challenging to demonstrate creativity when the opinion of your observer matters so much. Difficult as it may seem, a certain level of detachment from the outcome will aid the smooth running of your interactions with inspectors.

➤ It has been suggested that some headteachers insist that staff take a 'party line' when speaking to inspectors, rather than allowing them a free voice. While it is natural for teachers to discuss what they have been asked and how they replied, always remember that you have complete freedom to answer questions with honesty and integrity.

➤ When you are interacting with inspectors you are not live on *Newsnight*! If something occurs to you *after* a discussion, which would add to the impression that an inspector has of some aspect of your work, make a note of it and make sure that the inspector receives it, or arrange some time with the inspector to discuss this additional information. If this time is not granted, ensure that the registered inspector hears your views. Your headteacher will be in a position to facilitate this. Discussions with inspectors should not be 'now or never' affairs.

➤ If you know you have time set aside for a discussion with an inspector, make brief bullet points of what you wish to convey (for example, what you do particularly well). Hence, if you run out of time, you can give your inspector your notes for his or her later perusal.

➤ This should not occur, but if you feel you are being directed into giving a particular answer, restate the question back to the questioner and give the answer you want to give, rather than the one you feel directed to give. You could even say 'what is it that you are asking?'.

➤ There is no perfect way to teach. The dynamics of the personalities involved mean that only trial can reveal a good way for a particular class at a particular time. By making this view known to inspectors, you will be indicating your willingness to be flexible and respond to the needs of the moment in your class.

▶ Central to sound communication must be the ability to reciprocate. With full attention to, and assimilation of, what the other person has said, there can be little room for the obstacle of ineffective communication.

▶ Take a moment to consider how effective your listening skills are when communicating with colleagues and inspectors. Are you interested in what is said? What is your initial reaction to the speaker? Do you have any preconceptions that may block your ability to listen with freedom? Do you listen to what is being said, as well as what is not being said?

'When you undervalue what you do, the world will undervalue what you are.' SUZE ORMAN

'Hearing' feedback

'If the criticism is valid, it must be made.' NELSON MANDELA

When an inspector has observed your lessons and has reached certain conclusions about your performance, s/he will have to give you *constructive* feedback (usually done as soon as possible after the inspection). This feedback is given to full- and part-time teachers, supply teachers (unless they have worked for less than five days in the school), teachers funded under grants for specific purposes, and qualified support teachers. Feedback will not necessarily be offered to trainee teachers, nursery or classroom assistants, SEN support assistants, non-teaching assistants, artists or writers in residence, instructors and coaches, or any other voluntary support staff.

During these feedback sessions on individual performance, your inspector will aim to:

– *'identify the most important strengths and weaknesses in the teaching observed;*

– *provide clear reasons for what [the inspector] judged to be successful or otherwise;*

– *ensure that points for development are identified.'* [6]

The feedback you are offered must take place in total privacy and certainly *not* within earshot of pupils. You must be offered examples that back up the evaluations made by inspectors, as well as the opportunity to ask questions to ensure that the evaluations made have been understood. This is not as easy as it sounds, because human interaction between the two individuals involved can mean that what is meant is not always said, and what is said is not always heard! In addition to this, there is a tendency not to *absorb* all the information that is heard.

The main barriers to *hearing* feedback are:
- being preoccupied with the possible negatives;
- being preoccupied with the possible positives;
- feeling criticised or defensive;
- poor communication between you and your inspector (possibly the result of a poor relationship);
- feeling that your inspector does not have the ability (or even competence) to comment on your work.

Added to these possible barriers is the fact that each individual has a different capacity for receiving feedback, which can vary from one day to the next. So many factors influence this, such as health, mood, energy levels etc., that those offering feedback must have highly tuned skills of perceptiveness if maximum benefit is to be gained from the information they have to impart. Some business writers have compared these different capacities to *buckets, tumblers* and *thimbles*.

According to the publication *Constructive Feedback* [7] by the Institute of Personnel and Development:
- *buckets* seek out feedback, with confidence in their ability to improve;
- *tumblers* are happier with only three or four key pieces of information about their performance; and
- *thimbles* need careful nurturing through the process of feedback.

ACTION: Think about the way that you receive feedback. Would you describe yourself as a bucket, a tumbler or a thimble? Can you judge how full your bucket, tumbler or thimble *is already? Do you respond to feedback with action? Would you like to see changes in the way you receive feedback? How might those changes be brought about? Who is in the best position to help you?*

Inspectors are given guidance on how best to communicate findings to teachers. They are aware that they must gain each teacher's acceptance, and must show sensitivity in the way they deal with teachers and pupils. An enormous amount of skill is required of inspectors if the impact of what they have to say is to be positive.

That said, there are many non-verbal forms of communication that can 'speak' volumes. When you are experiencing an inspection, it is easy to allow your sensitivity to become heightened. Interactions with inspectors depend on mutually effective social and communication skills; if either party expresses dominance over the other, these interactions will be ultimately destructive.

From the inspectors' viewpoint, they are advised in *The Handbooks for Inspecting Schools* [8] that '*eye contact and appropriate facial expression, posture, gesture, voice, pace and tone can all help to reduce anxiety, gain acceptance of inspection findings and encourage constructive professional dialogue. Oral messages and body language should always be compatible.*'

ACTION: It can be helpful to consider your own posture, gesture, voice, pace and tone when interacting with inspectors. Does your voice change? Do you feel defensive or open? Would an inspector feel free to discuss the inspection with you? Is there action you can take to facilitate a free-flowing, two-way discussion between you and those inspecting you? Do you accept that the way you respond to feedback is fully in your power?

Disagreement is a perfectly normal part of life. When two humans interact, there are at least two points of view. There is nothing inherently bad about disagreement over feedback during an inspection, as long as steps are taken by both parties to reach a meaningful resolution. If this situation remains unmanaged, trust is destroyed and true communication breaks down.

There are three common reasons for feeling disgruntled about criticism.

1 **If you are criticised for something that you normally do well but happened not to when being observed by inspectors.**

   Do not feel that you should not make this clear to inspectors. There is nothing wrong with saying that what was witnessed is not your usual standard and even offering reasons for why you think this might have been the case.

2 **If you know that the criticism concerns an area of your work that you have already identified as being in need of further development.**

   Explain this to the inspector, and show any available evidence that you have already identified this development need. The final report should make a distinction between what has been detected by inspectors as a development need, and what has already been flagged up by your school's internal review and evaluation processes.

3 **If you are criticised for something that has been your area of responsibility for several years.**

   This is a tough one. It can be very hard to swallow such criticism, but if an inspector has the evidence to suggest that the criticism needs to be made, unfortunately there is nothing to be done other than facing the need for improvement. If you still feel that the criticism is unfair, and have sufficient evidence to support your view, speak to your headteacher about your next step. It may be appropriate to lodge a complaint with the registered inspector.

When feedback is not constructive

'No one can make you inferior without your consent.'
ELEANOR ROOSEVELT

While all inspectors will have received training in how to debrief teachers during an inspection, inevitably there will be some occasions when the feedback is not as constructive as it might be. There will be several contributing reasons for this, perhaps the most significant being that consistency cannot be guaranteed in any aspect of life.

The following ideas may help you to deal with feedback in the unlikely event that it is not being constructive:

ABOUT

THE PURPOSE OF FEEDBACK

▶ At its best, feedback can be a major source of positivity, allowing us to focus on what we have learnt and what we still have to develop. Both are valid and valuable lessons. We only need to consider what working life would be like without any feedback at all on performance; professional development would become an extremely haphazard affair!

▶ When you are listening to the feedback being offered to you by an inspector (or anyone else who may have observed your work), keep in mind the purpose of the exercise:

- You should be given conclusions about your performance that have been reached through comparing your work against objective standards.

- Feedback should enable you to further develop positivity about your work (a common belief is 'that which is recognised and rewarded is repeated').

- Feedback should encourage you to move towards targets for improvement and help you to realise your full potential.

▶ Feedback should not identify, or even highlight, major problem areas in your performance, because there are other systems in schools for this. It should never be a time of shock. If you come away from a feedback session remembering only the negative aspects, take care to appreciate the impact this is having on your other belief systems.

- Seek out what the person debriefing you *intends*. For example, is there any *positive* intent, or does it appear to be purely negative (which would be extremely unusual)?

- Feedback should be objective. If you sense that it has become subjective, state what you suspect may be happening. It would also be wise to ask for specific examples to illustrate the debriefing you are being given.

- Reflect back to the person debriefing you what you understand to be the key points from the feedback, but take care to use constructive, positive language.

- Aim to identify how you are thinking about the feedback you are receiving. Is it welcome? Do you feel positive about the person debriefing you? Is there anything in your thoughts that might be preventing you from viewing the feedback as constructive?

- Do be aware of the power of language. Regular subscribers to Usenet [9] will know how easily language can offend and how quickly some users resort to 'flaming' those who have touched a sensitive nerve! Is there any chance that you have been oversensitive in your interpretation of what has been said to you? Are there differences between your perceptions and those of your inspector?

- Remember that you can evaluate the feedback you have been given against what you know about the way you work, and also against other feedback received from within your school.

- If the feedback you receive really does seem to be lacking in constructive qualities, talk to your headteacher about the possibility of lodging a complaint. However, do not feel that you must simply 'put up with it'. Remember to write down in detail exactly what happened in your debriefing.

As well as offering feedback, your inspector will also give you a profile of the judgements on the quality of teaching in each of your lessons *that were observed*. These will be described as:

- excellent;
- very good (grades 1 and 2);
- good;
- satisfactory (grades 3 and 4);

- unsatisfactory;
- poor or very poor (grades 5, 6 and 7).

A copy of this profile will be given to your headteacher who should treat it in the strictest confidence. This judgement is not a summative evaluation of your professional competence. Being given a grade of 5, 6 or 7 should never be used to justify action against you by your school. However, if you do receive one of these grades, contact your union for advice.

Regardless of the nature of the feedback you receive during any debriefing sessions, you are likely to feel drained at the end of the inspection when you are given your profile of teaching. Do keep this in mind, as well as the possible need for some kind of relaxing treat that evening (one that certainly does not involve work!).

ABOUT

FEEDBACK IN SHORT INSPECTIONS

If your school receives a short inspection, you may not be observed at all. If you are observed, inspectors will endeavour to offer verbal feedback as they go along, but you will almost certainly not receive a summary feedback towards the end of the inspection. Profiles of inspectors' judgements on teaching will also not be given.

If you have management responsibility for a subject or other key area of your school's work, the feedback you receive will probably be 'drip-fed' throughout the inspection week. In theory, there is tremendous scope for a mutual sharing of hypotheses about the work of your team, and it would be wise to direct your inspector to areas of excellence and lessons that you know are sure to impress.

By the end of the inspection, you should have no doubts as to how well you and your team are performing. However, if differences of opinion have developed between you and your inspector, take the opportunity during feedback time to seek clarity on the conclusions that have been reached and to explore your differences thoroughly. This is not a time to listen and keep quiet! Challenge all assumptions that you feel do not reflect your work. Do not let the feedback session end without doing everything in your power either to reach an agreement, or to achieve mutual understanding of what your differences are and why they exist.

ABOUT

DIFFERENCES BETWEEN ORAL FEEDBACK AND WRITTEN PROFILES

▶ There is no doubt that differences between what is said and what is written about a teacher's performance can, and do, arise. It could be that the inspector is aiming to encourage the teacher through the inspection, or that s/he fears the response from the teacher if true feelings were spoken. Whatever the reason, this mismatch between oral and written feedback is fundamentally unprofessional but, sadly, extremely difficult to eradicate.

▶ If this is your experience, discuss the matter with your headteacher at the earliest opportunity. It may be necessary to lodge a complaint, especially if several teachers in your school share the same experience. Such a mismatch between oral and written feedback damages trust unnecessarily.

▶ Difficult as this may be, do all in your power not to let this destroy your confidence as the inspection draws to a close. You have experienced an important rite of passage in your career, and even if there is work still to be done, it is essential to take a step back, give yourself a breather and celebrate your successes (with others in your school, if possible), before focusing on future improvements.

It is not acceptable for your inspector to evade such a discussion. If this is your experience, lodge a complaint with your headteacher who should pass your feelings on to your registered inspector. Do not leave it there! Pursue this complaint as high as you need to until you receive a satisfactory result.

Whenever you receive feedback from an inspector, make sure you keep a written record of what has been said and by whom. This will prove invaluable if you ever have cause to lodge a complaint about the inspection, and will also help you to accept the positive as well as the negative aspects (provided that you always bear the positive ones in mind).

Coping with stress during the inspection experience

You have made it through the pre-inspection stages, so this really is a time to enjoy the fruits of your labour. If, however, you find yourself experiencing negative stress as the week begins, do not simply ignore it. There are plenty of techniques to employ to enable you to flourish during the inspection. If you do not respond to these self-help techniques, it is very important to seek the advice of your chosen healthcare provider. Ask for a telephone consultation if you cannot get an appointment. See also the sections on stress busting on pages 87–8 and 151–5.

Some self-help remedies have a proven record of benefit, and are included below:

- Bach Rescue Remedy is great for quick results. Either put four drops directly on your tongue, or into a small quantity of water which can be sipped at regular intervals.

- The Homoeopathic remedy *Argentum Nitricum* has a great track record for those who feel they are suffering from internal turmoil. Low potencies are available from high street pharmacies, but it is usually best to visit a qualified practitioner so that you take the potency most suited to you.

- Remember to eat little and often. This will help you maintain healthy blood sugar levels. If these fluctuate too wildly, you may feel more stressed than you really are.

- Book a stress busting treatment (such as a massage) early in the week. Do not feel that you cannot afford the time – an hour of pure relaxation is sure to increase your productivity in the long run.

- Talk to colleagues about their experiences. They may be able to offer you some valuable perspective. You may even realise that you are coping better than anyone else! Utilise your school's support systems (many headteachers now set aside time during the inspection week in which to listen to the concerns and stresses of staff members).

- Try not to attach yourself to a particular outcome. The inspection has arrived, and what will be will be. Trust that the judgements made will be accurate, and remember that if you feel this is not the case there are steps you can take to make your feelings known. Inspection does not have to threaten your health and well-being – it is only a temporary situation.

- Do not forget to breathe; not the way you usually breathe, but taking slow, deep breaths that allow you physically to relax. See pages 154, 170 for an easy breathing exercise.

EXAMPLE: My experience of two inspections is that anxiety of the unknown often dominates teachers' thoughts. One way we dealt with this was to have a roster of governors during the inspection week. There was always a governor in the school every day from 8.00 a.m. until 6.00 p.m.; their task was to be a sounding board, to help if there was a problem, and to be totally supportive. Governors did not interfere, but our presence was noticed by the inspectors. Indeed, as chairman of governors, I went out of my way to tell the registered inspector what our plans were. This presence certainly helped. It enabled me to go to the registered inspector to help sort out a misunderstanding before it became a real problem.

Making complaints

'Every kind of peaceful co-operation among men is primarily based on mutual trust and only secondarily on institutions such as courts of justice and police.' ALBERT EINSTEIN

It should be acknowledged that the vast majority of school inspections are carried out without cause for complaint. Nevertheless, there are set procedures for lodging complaints about an inspection. These are laid out in Figure 4.1 overleaf.

In brief, any teacher in your school can raise concerns with your headteacher. S/he will then discuss with the registered inspector how this might be resolved. If an agreement cannot be reached, the complaint can be referred to the contractor. Should the contractor fail to resolve the issue satisfactorily, your headteacher can then send a formal written complaint to Ofsted.

If this does not solve the issue, the complaint will be referred to the Ofsted Complaints Adjudicator. The final resting-place for unresolved complaints is the Ombudsman (Parliamentary Commissioner for Administration). To date, very few complaints have reached the Ofsted Complaints Adjudicator and Ombudsman.

Making complaints *before* an inspection

Before inspectors have arrived at your school, any complaints you may have are likely to be related to the way in which pre-inspection procedures have been managed by the inspection team. Complaints at this stage are unusual but must be resolved with great skill on the part of both the contractor/inspection team and your school, if the inspection is not to be tainted by a bad start and loss of mutual trust.

Whatever the reason for your complaint, the following steps will ensure that you do everything in your power to reach a resolution:

1 Obtain and read copies of *Making Complaints to Ofsted* and *Ofsted Complaints Adjudicator*, both available free of charge from the Ofsted Publications Centre on tel. no. 020 7510 0180. These publications will

Figure 4.1: Formal Complaints Procedure for Schools

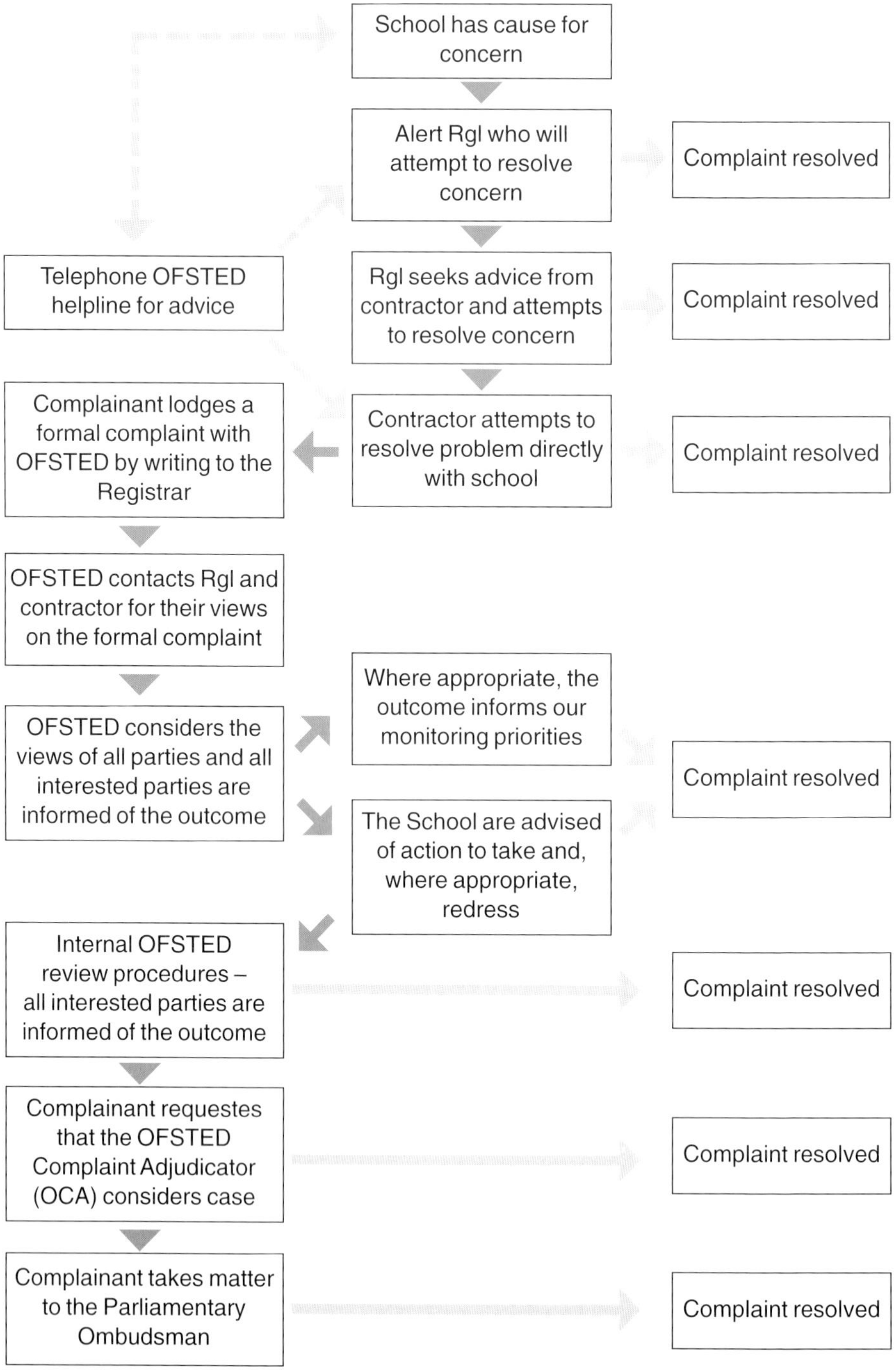

School has cause for concern

↓

Alert Rgl who will attempt to resolve concern → Complaint resolved

↓

Telephone OFSTED helpline for advice

Rgl seeks advice from contractor and attempts to resolve concern → Complaint resolved

↓

Complainant lodges a formal complaint with OFSTED by writing to the Registrar ← Contractor attempts to resolve problem directly with school → Complaint resolved

↓

OFSTED contacts Rgl and contractor for their views on the formal complaint

↓

OFSTED considers the views of all parties and all interested parties are informed of the outcome

Where appropriate, the outcome informs our monitoring priorities → Complaint resolved

The School are advised of action to take and, where appropriate, redress

↓

Internal OFSTED review procedures – all interested parties are informed of the outcome → Complaint resolved

↓

Complainant requestes that the OFSTED Complaint Adjudicator (OCA) considers case → Complaint resolved

↓

Complainant takes matter to the Parliamentary Ombudsman → Complaint resolved arm you with the knowledge you need in order to ensure that any complaints you have cause to make are lodged in the correct way. The latest Annual Report of the Ofsted Complaints Adjudicator will make interesting reading, too.

2   Someone in your school will have the responsibility of receiving concerns and complaints about the inspection. This will usually be your headteacher, although this unenviable task may be delegated to a deputy in large schools. Make sure that you raise your concerns with the appropriate person. Your complaint should be dealt with confidentially, and you should also be offered the assurance that a satisfactory solution will be sought.

3   Keep a written record of any complaints you lodge, and of any discussion regarding the complaint. Include as much evidence as you can about why you feel it is necessary to make this complaint, and what you have done personally to facilitate a solution. Such a record will prove invaluable in the unlikely event of the complaint being referred to the Ofsted Complaints Adjudicator, or beyond.

4   Air even the smallest of grievances to the appropriate person in your school; this is far better than letting them fester and eat away your positivity and enthusiasm. Also, let your union representative know what you are doing, in case the need for union involvement arises.

5   Attend all pre-inspection meetings so that you have all the information you require in order to prepare for a successful inspection. Ask for clarification on any aspect of the process that remains unclear.

6   Once you have raised a complaint to be dealt with, do not let it drop. Too often teachers report that they do not find out the consequences of the complaints they make, and this is a pitiful state of affairs. If your headteacher has raised the issue with your registered inspector, s/he should get back to you with a breakdown of how the situation was, or will be, resolved. **Do not, under any circumstances, lose track of what happens and resign yourself to not hearing the result of your complaint.**

7   If your registered inspector is unable to resolve the issue, it must be referred to the contractor who must, in turn, have procedures set up to deal with complaints from schools. If a school is still not happy with the way in which the complaint has been handled, the complaint can then be referred to Ofsted and beyond.

Making complaints *during* an inspection

Once the inspection has started, you should still feel free to express any concerns you may have about the way it is being conducted. Feedback and complaints are ways in which Ofsted and contractors can find out about the actual delivery of inspections. In the past, changes were made to the way that inspections are performed, as a result of complaints from those on the receiving end; thus, if you have a point to make, be sure to make it.

Your registered inspector is the person responsible for ensuring that the inspection runs smoothly with the maximum satisfaction (on the part of the school) possible. S/he will be in daily contact with your headteacher to discuss any issues that have cropped up, and a complaint would be just such an issue.

- As soon as you feel you have cause to complain, do not waste any time in discussing the matter with your headteacher (or whoever has the responsibility for receiving complaints from staff). Keep a written record of all events relating to your complaint.

- If the matter is not resolved as a result of this discussion, request that it be raised with the registered inspector. Make sure you ask to be advised on how the discussion went.

- If the matter is still not resolved, go back to your headteacher to discuss the possibility of raising your complaint with the inspection contractor.

- The next steps would be to lodge a formal written complaint with Ofsted itself, but this should be done only if your registered inspector and contractor cannot resolve the matter. In most cases, this final step would not be taken while the inspection was still taking place.

It is essential that you are kept fully informed of the progress of your complaint. Do not feel that once you have expressed your opinion you have no right to know what the verdict is. If you hear nothing within a reasonable amount of time, request to be informed of what the situation is at the earliest opportunity. Do not drop your complaint until you are happy with the conclusion. This may take effort and energy, but will avoid the feeling that there is *no* redress. Moreover, the fact that you are prepared to persist to the bitter end sends very clear messages to those with responsibilities for inspection. Mistakes are sometimes made during inspections, and it is far better for all involved that any such mistakes are dealt with in a spirit of openness. The Ofsted leaflet *Making Complaints to Ofsted* (available from the publications centre on tel. no. 020 510 0180) will be useful.

ABOUT

THE IMPORTANCE OF MAKING COMPLAINTS

❯ If you were to go into a high street store, receive shoddy treatment, poor quality goods and have to wait in queues that wrap around the shop, you would probably consider making a complaint. What's more, that store, if it is ambitious and mindful of performance, will welcome comments from customers so that improvements in service can be addressed.

❯ It is through receiving complaints that companies and organisations are in a position to improve performance. If you are not totally happy with the way in which your inspection is carried out, it is really important to identify exactly what it is that you are not happy with, and to discuss this with your headteacher with a view to taking the complaint further. By not making your feelings known, changes cannot be brought about as a result of your experience, which is a wasted opportunity as well as being demoralising for you.

❯ Inspection policy can be (and has been) influenced by the complaints of teachers. Complaints are one way of providing a check and balance on how inspectors (and the inspection system itself) are performing. Indeed, Ofsted welcomes complaints, viewing them as '*an important part of our own quality assurance measures*'.[10]

1   TSO, 1999.

2   *The Handbooks for Inspecting Schools*, TSO, 1999.

3   *Inspecting Schools, the Framework*, effective from January 2000, Ofsted.

4   *The Other Side of the Dale* and *Over Hill and Dale*, both published by Penguin.

5   Arrow, 1999.

6   *The Handbooks for Inspecting Schools*, TSO, 1999.

7   By Roland and Frances Bee.

8   TSO, 1999.

9   Usenet is the collective term for Internet Newsgroups.

10 *Making Complaints to Ofsted*, 1998.

CHAPTER 5

Role of the teacher

Characteristics of an effective teacher

Measuring effectiveness (along with efficiency and value for money) is central to Ofsted's reason for being. As far as the inspection is concerned, the way you teach and the way your pupils learn will be analysed closely (see Chapter 3, The Evaluation Schedule).

Much has been written on teacher effectiveness; some of it is extremely useful and some is quite unachievable. Below is a brief summary of a selection of the main ideas on effectiveness from those in the classroom. Use them to trigger improvements in any areas of your work that you feel may benefit. Again, talking to a trusted colleague who has the privilege of knowing your work well will be beneficial. This is one way in which your professional mind can be focused by an inspection, and the possibilities for gain and benefit are great. Try not to pass up this opportunity.

Effectiveness must be empowering. If there is too much emphasis on the bureaucracy of *proving* effectiveness, the result will be burdensome disempowerment. Underpinning effectiveness must be an ongoing drive for improvement. However, to seek *perfection* simultaneously in all aspects of your work is ultimately self-destructive. Be mindful of any need you may have to pursue perfection, and what impact this has on your self-esteem, self-acceptance and work. Beware of the paralysing effects of the perfection pursuit!

It would be impossible to create checklists for a self-evaluation of effectiveness for all teachers of all subjects. However, there are some generic areas of the job that do lend themselves to such a summary, and these are discussed below.

When considering teacher effectiveness, the most important thing to remember is that there is no person on this planet who can sustain a high level of effectiveness indefinitely. This is because effectiveness is bound to fluctuate, depending on the pressures you are under and the dynamics of your classroom relationships at any given time. However, with the skills of intuition (to sense the 'mood' of the class) and responsiveness (to enable you to make quick decisions about the pace and content of your lessons), the chances of your working with effectiveness are dramatically increased. In short, effectiveness is about the opportunities you provide in your classroom for learning to take place; very little else matters.

Through experience, most teachers create useful habits of self-evaluation to promote effectiveness in the classroom, and many such teachers have been willing to share their ideas for this book. These ideas are offered below in the spirit of comradeship! Use them as points to consider, rather than a formula for the perfect way to teach, or a 'model' for evaluation (there is little point in 'cloning' teachers). There is no such thing as a teacher who is considered to be 'great' by all those that s/he comes into contact with.

Effectiveness in the classroom

The key questions for the teacher to consider here are as follows (see also Table 5.1):

- Is my classroom a learning environment?
- Do my pupils know exactly what standards of behaviour are expected of them? Do they follow established routines in my classroom? Do I know and use their names? Do I catch children doing something *right* or something *wrong*?
- Is my subject knowledge good? Am I able to show this in the way I present my subject(s) and in discussions?
- Do my pupils know what objectives I am aiming for? Do they know at the beginning of each lesson what and how I want them to learn? Can they apply what they learn to real-life situations?

- Can I challenge and inspire pupils, keeping them working at a good pace? Do I notice what they do well? Do I use appropriate differentiation? Do they stay on task? Are my lessons inescapable?

- Do I have high expectations of *every* pupil? Do they all cover the same *range* of work? Do they have personal motivational targets for learning (perhaps written down somewhere for easy reference)? Are my pupils *hopeful*?

- Can I vary my teaching methods depending on the needs of each class? Can I identify what methods can achieve greatest success? Do I *demonstrate*?

- Do I vary my questioning techniques to enable pupils of all abilities to take part in each stage of every lesson? Do I vary the tone, pitch and pace of my voice to help facilitate understanding? Do I use questioning to check levels of understanding?

- Do I use homework as a way of reinforcing what I teach? Is this tailored to individual needs? Does it promote independent learning? Can I offer advice on independent reading on the topic being taught?

- Do I promote concentration by keeping noise in my lessons to a minimum?

- Do pupils have the opportunity to develop *skills* in my lessons? Can pupils apply intellectual, physical or creative effort when tackling the work I set? Are my pupils *interested* in the work they do in my lessons? Do I nurture imaginative thinking? Do I encourage independent problem-solving?

- Can I make improvements in the way I structure my lessons? Would more in-depth research add value to my lessons?

- How perceptive am I to the changing needs of my pupils? Are my pupils eager to push their boundaries of extended learning? Does every lesson push us closer towards our goals? Are my pupils confident enough to work independently? Do they feel responsible for their learning?

- Do I connect the threads of new learning with old? Do I explain follow-on objectives?

- Do my pupils respond to my explanations of new concepts and topics?

- Do the resources I use add to the depth of learning and understanding amongst my pupils?

- Are my intentions met in my lessons? Do my pupils know how they will be evaluated and assessed? Do I review what has been taught at the end of each lesson?

- Are any practical activities that my pupils engage in purposeful – or even memorable? Do my pupils feel that they have choices? Can they problem-solve?

- Do I liaise with the SEN co-ordinator and local education authority SEN staff when appropriate? Do I use support staff to full effect?

- Do the contributions of *all* my pupils matter equally? Do pupils *feel* successful?

- Am I a 'leader' in my classroom, or do I resort to 'authority'?

ABOUT

EFFECTIVE TEACHING

Ofsted has summarised what it considers to be important factors in effective teaching. These are reproduced below (Table 5.1) and can also be found in the Ofsted booklet *Lessons Learned from Special Measures*.

Table 5.1: Important factors in effective teaching

Questioning	Assessing	Exposition to the whole class	Using additional adults
Listening	Reminding		
Explaining	Describing	Summarising work covered	Providing suitable resources
Demonstrating	Guiding		
Instructing	Reading aloud	Setting homework	
Managing	Practical work by pupils		Knowing the pupils' needs
Challenging		Correcting mistakes	
Praising	Working with small groups		Evaluating lessons

ACTION: Think about what you consider to be the best conditions for effective learning. Is there anything lacking in the conditions that you find yourself working in, and those that you have created? Can you influence or effect improvements in those conditions?

ABOUT

LESSON PLANS

The Ofsted booklet *Lessons Learned from Special Measures* includes a summary of what effective lesson plans include (reproduced below). Even though your school may be far from requiring special measures, it can be useful to refer to the following checklist from time to time.

Effective lesson plans include:

- Clear learning objectives;
- Approximate timings for each part of the lesson;
- Activities which relate to the learning objective;
- The subject-specific language to be used;
- The deployment of, and tasks for, additional adults;
- Briefing notes for support staff and others;
- Special resources that are needed for that lesson;
- Indication of where work is differentiated;
- Assessment details for individuals, groups or the whole class;
- Evaluation notes;
- Information for use in the next lesson.

EXAMPLE: However carefully we prepare our lessons for an inspection, they stand or fall, like all lessons, on our ability to hold pupils' interest. We do this through projecting our own personalities as we present the material – very much as professional entertainers project theirs. Unfortunately, we do not have a front-of-house manager to maintain order among the audience; we have to do this at the same time as giving our performance. We have to develop relationships with pupils as individuals and as a group, and all human relationships are dynamic. We cannot predict the mood our pupils will be in on any given day, yet we have to be ready to respond at all times in a quick-thinking, positive and mature way. In order to meet the demands of the classroom, we need to draw on all our best qualities, all our energy.

Effectiveness in administration

The key questions for the teacher to consider in the context of administration are as follows:

- Is my planning effective in covering objectives?
- Do I assess pupils' achievements in a way that enables me to indicate how difficulties can be overcome, and how further improvements might be made? Do I have all the necessary guidelines/policies/documentation for marking pupils' work?
- Do I distinguish between *standards* and *attainment*?
- Am I in a position to identify my strengths and development needs?
- Can I identify patterns in the way that my pupils perform? Can I analyse and conceptualise possible solutions to this? Am I decisive? Do my assessments fall in line with National Curriculum results? Do I use internal moderation to guard against over- or under-marking?
- Am I organised in my work? Is storage and retrieval of information easy?
- Can I respond promptly to the administration needs of others (for example, when asked for information or paperwork)?

❭ In order to make progress, the would-be accomplished flautist must practise arpeggios and heptatonic, pentatonic, chromatic and diminished scales (among others), painstakingly listening to the tone and quality of each note, returning to the start if it wavers or loses clarity. Regardless of how beautifully each tune is played, or how imaginatively music is created, without this constant and repetitive focus on the fundamentals of flute playing, real progress cannot be harnessed with consistency.

❭ To a great extent, these principles apply to just about every aspect of life. While it may seem tiresome (and possibly also irritating that it should even be suggested) to focus on the minutiae of our jobs from time to time, the result can only be positive!

Effectiveness in working relationships

In terms of working relationships, the questions to consider are:

● Have I provided a positive atmosphere in which my pupils can work?

● Are my pupils happy to consult me about any aspect of their work or emotional well-being? Can I freely confront poor performance? Do I use choice to divert poor behaviour? Are parents/carers happy to consult me with any concerns? Am I fair and consistent?

● Do I work effectively with colleagues? Do support staff know how I would like them to work? Do I share goals with colleagues? Do I request feedback from those who know my work? Do I offer feedback to colleagues when asked? Do I feel part of a team? Am I willing to be flexible? Do I share my good ideas? Am I free to discuss opinions that I might disagree with?

● Am I sensitive to the moods of my pupils and colleagues? Can I nurture sensitivity and understanding in others? Am I free to understand *why* people may be feeling as they are?

● Do my colleagues know how I feel about issues affecting staff? Do I contribute to staff meetings?

ABOUT

ASSESSING YOUR EFFECTIVENESS

❯ When thinking about your effectiveness and assessing it against some of the points included above, do not fret if you identify areas for development. As mentioned before, there is no such thing as the 'perfect' teacher – the 'human' teacher, yes; but 'perfect', no! In fact, to have identified areas for development for yourself is usually a bonus as far as inspection is concerned; what better way to show that you are a truly reflective practitioner?

❯ If the development needs you have flagged up are brought up in your feedback sessions with an inspector, s/he *should* acknowledge that you had identified them first.

❯ It might be an idea to inform your curriculum or year leader, or your senior management team, if you have identified development needs in addition to what your school's internal performance management procedures have identified. Keep a written record of discussions on how these needs will be met for future reference, should the time or support for necessary development not be forthcoming.

❯ Do not view effectiveness as a linear process – it is far more complex than that. There is no magic formula to improve effectiveness; it is simply a matter of identifying, and focusing on, issues within the context in which you work.

Hay McBer report of research into teacher effectiveness

In June 2000, Hay McBer published a model of teacher effectiveness. The descriptions of effective teachers were based on evidence of what effective teachers do in practice. The introduction of this report states that '*Effective teachers in the future will need to deal with a climate of continual change in which distance learning and other teaching media will become more prevalent. The 'star' teachers of the future will be those who work to make what is now the best become the standard for all.*'[1]

With this in mind, it is hoped that the research will take its place '*in the strategy of modernising the teaching profession by supporting a whole range of management processes deployed within schools: performance management, selection, career planning and professional development'.*

This book cannot provide the space to include an extensive overview of this research. Suffice to say that it supports the often-held view that it is the interconnected factors of professional characteristics, teaching skills and classroom climate that combine to contribute to the overall effectiveness of a teacher. Do obtain a copy of this report (available on the DfEE website). It is food for thought; your school, as part of its performance management, may well adopt this model of effectiveness characteristics.

At least be aware, as you prepare for inspection, of the *Dictionary of Characteristics* that the report identifies for classroom teachers on the main professional grade, teachers at the threshold and outstanding teachers. These characteristics have been summarised below (Table 5.2):

Table 5.2: Summary of characteristics of effective teachers

Professionalism	Leading
Challenge and support	Flexibility
Confidence	Holding people accountable
Creating trust	Managing pupils
Respect for others	Passion for learning

Thinking	Relating to others
Analytical thinking	Impact and influence
Conceptual thinking	Teamworking
	Understanding others

Planning and setting expectations	
Drive for improvement	
Information seeking	
Initiative	

Self-evaluation of lessons and peer observation

'It is one of the most beautiful compensations of life that no man can sincerely try to help another without helping himself.'

RALPH WALDO EMERSON

Ongoing self-evaluation (of standards as well as teaching) seems to be one of the most effective ways of maintaining success in the classroom and *'nibbling away at priorities'*[2]. While it would be impracticable to evaluate every lesson, it is a good idea to get into, or retain, the habit of periodic review of your work in the classroom. It can also be helpful to discuss with older children at the end of a lesson:

a What is the most significant piece of information that they are taking away with them?

b What aspect of the lesson would they like to know more about?

The Handbooks for Inspecting Schools state that:

The overriding consideration for evaluating the quality of teaching is how well pupils learn. This is judged not only by assessing their knowledge, understanding and skills, but by looking at the extent of their engagement in the lesson, the pace of their work and the demands made of them... Evaluation and setting an agenda for development are starting points, but are of limited value unless the monitoring of classroom teaching is systematic; carried out to agreed criteria; and the outcomes discussed with teachers.

Some schools have excellent internal systems in place for staff self-review and peer observation. If your school does not have them, it may be worth getting together with a trusted colleague and arranging them yourself. Governors can be useful here! As 'critical friends', they can ask pertinent questions of the how/what/when/why variety, and achieve the double goal of becoming familiar with exactly what goes on in your school's classrooms. (Do not forget that governors come under scrutiny during an inspection, and some may never have observed a lesson in progress before. Visiting the classroom is one way of monitoring and evaluating school and teacher effectiveness.)

There are several methods of observation to use that will facilitate useful feedback. It would be worthwhile spending a little time devising a *proforma* for your needs. Table 5.3 illustrates a checklist that is used by Worthing High School with good outcomes. It was developed by a

Table 5.3: Checklist for lesson evaluation

Did I...	
Introduce the lesson?	YES/NO
Put the lesson in context?	YES/NO
Make sure the pupils listened in silence?	YES/NO
Introduce the key words to be used?	YES/NO

Did I...	
Maintain the pace of the lesson?	YES/NO
Maintain high expectations?	YES/NO
Differentiate the tasks appropriately?	YES/NO
Regularly interact with the pupils?	YES/NO

Were the pupils...	
On task?	YES/NO
Actively engaged in their learning?	YES/NO
Aware of when they could talk or when they should remain silent?	YES/NO

Did I...	
Respond to previous homework?	YES/NO
Set homework?	YES/NO
Make sure that the homework task was clearly understood?	YES/NO
Make sure that all pupils entered the task into their organiser?	YES/NO
Set a deadline for completion?	YES/NO
Provide differentiated opportunities?	YES/NO

Finally, did I...	
Re-state the learning intentions?	YES/NO
Summarise what had been achieved?	YES/NO
Explain the intentions for the next lesson?	YES/NO
Ensure that pupils were focused and listening in silence?	YES/NO

(Adapted from NQT Handbook, p. 174)

group of West Sussex teachers, and is based on Alastair Smith's *Accelerated Learning Cycle*. This checklist could be used either for self-evaluation or, with a little adaptation, when observing a colleague's work in the classroom.

When observing colleagues, it is worth remembering a few important points to ensure that this powerful tool is used to its greatest advantage:

1 Make sure that the lesson to be observed is mutually convenient. That said, it is probably not a good idea only to observe a colleague teaching his or her favourite class, so perhaps encourage the observation of challenging classes.

2 Agree beforehand what form the observation and feedback will take, and arrange a specific time in which to discuss it. Just a few brief words straight after the lesson will not suffice. Think, also, about the spirit of the observation. Make sure that you both approach the exercise as equals.

3 Discuss in advance any concerns that the teachers you will be observing may have. For example, they may want some feedback on their voice control or pace, differentiation of work, etc. Discuss whether or not you will identify areas for development together.

4 Identify beforehand *low, average* and *high* attainers you might wish to focus on in the group. This will enable you to consider both the teaching *and* the learning. Perhaps devise a *proforma* for the observation of these children, so that you can make specific notes.

5 Consider how *you* feel when you are being observed. Are there any negative factors that you can avoid when observing others?

6 Be mindful of your own prejudices. Do you have preoccupations with how a lesson should be taught and behaviour managed, which are perhaps clouding your judgement of alternative options available? Are you able to be totally objective? Create an atmosphere of mutual trust and mutual respect.

7 Aim to observe the whole lesson. If this is not possible, stay for as long as you can.

8 Agree your observation criteria beforehand; for example, the lesson evaluation in Table 5.3. Alternatively, Ofsted's Evidence Forms may prove useful (see *The Handbooks for Inspecting Schools*).

9 Think about whether it is necessary to explain to pupils what you are doing in their lesson. Do try to avoid being a classroom assistant while in the room, tempting as it may be!

10 When giving feedback, think in terms of offering information, rather than criticising. Perhaps employ the time-tested method of offering statements of fact on what you witnessed during the lesson, rather than making actual judgements. This can be equally useful to the observed individuals, as they can draw their own conclusions about how their skills might be tightened up simply by having this information presented to them. If you do find it necessary to make what might be perceived as a negative point, sandwich it between two positives! Do be aware, though, that you will certainly do your colleague a disservice if your evaluation is not honest.

11 Relate feedback to the lesson plan and the learning objectives.

12 Are there any causes and effects that you can identify? Why was it that the lesson and learning outcomes were as they were?

13 Make the observation a two-way experience: for every lesson of a colleague that you observe, allow him or her to return the favour.

There can be few who would disagree with the view that a school filled with staff who regularly and effectively self-appraise/review has little use for an inspection report. By knowing that pupils depend heavily on the quality of teaching they are offered, staff can weave new strategies for improvement into their everyday work; strategies that draw on the experience of reflection and the desire to improve. Even Ofsted itself would wish this were so, and states in *The Handbooks for Inspecting Schools* that:

> *The school that knows and understands itself is well on the way to solving any problems it has. The school that is ignorant of its weaknesses, or will not, or cannot, face up to them, is not well managed. Self-evaluation provides the key to improvement.*

Self-evaluation is a major part of professional maturity, *engaging* teachers in what can be improved. If it becomes entrenched in the habits of our schools, then inspections will be relegated to an occasional, relatively minor, event which complements a school's internal assessments of its work.

School self-evaluation in a nutshell according to Ofsted

- Start now;
- Accept that we can all improve;
- Place the raising of standards at the heart of all your planning;
- Measure standards;
- Compare yourself with others;
- Regularly observe each other teaching to a set of agreed and rigorous criteria;
- Evaluate the effect that teaching has on learning;
- Be completely open in feeding back what you find;
- Think, discuss and consult;
- Set targets for everyone's improvement;
- Ensure that action is supported, monitored and reviewed;
- Never stop evaluating. [3]

'An activity becomes creative when the doer cares about doing it right, or doing it better.' JOHN UPDIKE

EXAMPLE: Our staff were very upbeat because they were proactive in monitoring and evaluating their own performance, anyway. The inspection itself was not without incident – one teacher fled in tears when a pupil was particularly bad in playing up to the stranger in the corner. However, staff had already identified that the disciplinary policy they had previously produced needed supporting by staff training in assertiveness techniques. Inspectors concentrated on such self-awareness and preparedness rather more than the tearful incidents, and we came out with a glowing report. So, the moral is, have faith in your own professionalism and do not expect to be superhuman.

Teacher's role in the preparation

'A thing is complete when you can let it be.' GITA BELLIN

There is no doubt that you will have some role to play in your school's preparation for inspection. The extent of your involvement will probably depend on the position that you hold within your school's hierarchy. Obviously, department/curriculum leaders, year heads, members of the senior management team, etc. will have specific focal points in the lead-up to an inspection, but every member of your school's community will be involved to some extent.

While you may have your own personal goals for preparation (perhaps to sort through your classroom or office space thoroughly, or to revamp some displays) just before an inspection is *not* the time to begin rewriting policies or creating documents. Such frenzied activity can only have a detrimental effect on your normal working duties, and add to the fatigue and depletion in morale that can be felt after an inspection. Ofsted is very keen to get across its message that extra preparation work *should not* be undertaken, and that it is perfectly acceptable for any document development needs to be flagged up for *future* focus, but not for cobbling together before inspectors arrive. For long-term use and value to a school, an inspection must come from everyday experience, not from having to change up a gear simply to 'get through'.

Of course, teachers want to present the best impression of their work possible – this is only natural. Realistically, you may be undertaking more in terms of preparing finely detailed lesson plans and perhaps more extravagant lesson resources. Additional administrative chores are unlikely to slot into your schedule without exerting pressure elsewhere in your working day (or, worse, extending your working day long into what should be your 'off duty' time). Moreover, keep in mind the widely held belief that 80 per cent of results stem from spending 20 per cent of your time on activities such as planning, building relationships and recreation.

The whole point of a visit from inspectors is so that they can assess the work of your school *as it stands*. There is little value in being given a particular conclusion on your work if it is not representative of what you could sustain on a day-to-day basis.

If you are asked to undertake additional preparation above what you would need to do to ensure that your own 'house' is in order, it may be necessary to tread a little carefully in reaching a solution. The very fact that additional work is being expected of you reveals that those doing the asking are feeling under pressure themselves. Ofsted is well aware that schools do sometimes over-prepare for inspection, and this knowledge helped to support the recent revisions to the *Framework for Inspection*.

NQT teachers

If you are an NQT teacher and are being asked to perform additional duties (perhaps covering for colleagues while they undertake inspection preparation), make sure that you discuss any concerns you may have with your induction tutor/mentor. Your guaranteed non-contact time should not be affected during the run-up to an inspection. If you still feel that undue pressures are being exerted, your union will be a source of support. You do not have to go through your school representative, if you would rather be advised by someone who was not a colleague – there should be a regional or national advisor who would respect your reasons for not wanting to raise such concerns within your school.

You should also discuss with your induction tutor/mentor any additional work you may want to carry out in order to get your records and planning in order (this may well be unnecessary). As an NQT, your experience of inspection will be no different from that of more established teachers. You do, however, have the distinct advantage of being used to observation while teaching, and familiar with talking about why you are working in a particular way.

Non-NQT teachers

For all other teachers, if you have a specific role to play in the run-up to an inspection, this should be discussed and *agreed* with you at the earliest possible stage. You should not have additional tasks sprung on you at short notice. Remember that your priority should be what you need to do in terms of lesson planning and making explicit to the inspectors the quality of your teaching. If other tasks are likely to squeeze your own preparation, you may want to discuss how necessary they are. Again, your union should be a source of support, as will Teacherline.

An unfortunate fact of life as a teacher is that it is often the super-efficient ones who are given additional tasks! Eventually, this can lead to a decline in performance, not to mention the onset of resentment, so do try to avoid this from happening. Be aware of the possibility of rising stress levels, and say 'no' if only for the sake of self-preservation. Remember that saying 'yes' means saying 'no' to something else.

Restrict yourself only to two pre-inspection goals at a time. Identify what they are and write down brief points on when you will know if your goal has been reached. It would be hopeless to attempt to focus on more than two goals at a time, because your normal work is bound to suffer and your mind will soar into overload.

Balance preparation for inspection with your normal workload by allocating your time in specific slots.

EXAMPLE: I was determined, second time around, not to get into the state I had before the first time I was inspected. I wanted to keep up with my usual workload, so I allocated time for inspection preparation. Where possible, I reduced my usual workload by setting homework that did not require intensive marking on my part. Then I spent just half an hour a day on preparation for inspection. This strategy worked well as everything felt contained, and I actually approached the inspection more laid-back than anyone else!

KNOWING THE EXTENT OF YOUR JOB

You will be expected to know exactly what your duties and responsibilities are, should an inspector choose to question you. Although this may seem obvious (you know what your job entails), just re-acquainting yourself with the full spectrum of the expectations that are made of you is worth the time.

Ask yourself these questions:

- Do you have a written job description (one that is up to date and truly reflects your work)? Do you have a copy?
- What are your additional responsibilities (such as being a tutor)?
- Have you read your pupils' records? Can you show that you know all you should know about them?
- Can you show that you follow your school's assessment and marking policies? If your school does not have such policies, do you have your own written policies which could stand up to scrutiny? Would you be able to demonstrate consistency?
- Do you know exactly what your school's specific targets are?
- Do you know the procedures for raising child protection issues? Who is your school's 'responsible' staff member? Who is your local education authority's responsible officer? What are the signs of possible abuse (your school's responsible staff member will be able to give you an outline of this)?
- Do you know and use your school's homework policy?
- How are your pupils with special educational needs cared for? Do you know your school's specific policy in this regard?
- Do you know and adhere to your school's bullying policy?
- Do you know and adhere to your school's behaviour policy?
- What are your literacy, numeracy and ICT responsibilities?
- What are your responsibilities towards ensuring equal opportunities for your pupils?

ABOUT

KNOWING THE EXTENT OF YOUR JOB continued

● Are you aware of your place in the grand scheme of things within your school? Who would you turn to with questions relating to any of the above issues? Who are your immediate curriculum/pastoral leaders? Is there a distinct line of management in your school – a 'chain of command' that must be followed, or can you receive support and advice from anyone, at any time?

If you need help with anything, ask for it *specifically*. A direct request is most likely to bring about the result or assistance you want. You should aim to be a supportive team member, not a carthorse carrying the burdens of all others!

The shared vision for your school should be a successful inspection, but the cost of this cannot, and should not, be weeks of intensive preparation. Success should be your school's reason for being, not a temporary desire brought about by a last-minute panic.

EXAMPLE: The main thing is to make sure that teachers still have time to get homework marked and returned to pupils, and that lessons still go ahead. For instance, one of my teachers is a senior member of staff and is in charge of arranging cover for absent teachers and a million other little jobs. He has been under a lot of pressure recently, and sometimes the headteacher has called him away from our classes so that they can check things. For a final year class (I am in year 13) I think this is bad.

Spiritual, moral, social and cultural development

'We need human qualities such as moral scruples, compassion and humility… These qualities are accessible only through forceful individual development.' HIS HOLINESS THE DALAI LAMA

This is an extremely complex area of education to assess and make judgements on. It is also an area in which many teachers pride themselves, despite the fact that these aspects of education are rarely planned as scrupulously as other subjects are. The other side of this coin, sadly, can be bafflement at what a teacher and the school as a whole are supposed to do to ensure that pupils receive this vital development.

Spiritual, moral, social and cultural development cannot happen if left to chance; pupils cannot be relied upon to 'catch' this education merely through example and observation! Pupils that are fearful of sanctions as a result of antisocial behaviour is no proof of social (or any other) development.

Some proponents of spiritual, moral, social and cultural development in schools believe that through every interaction with staff members, in every lesson and every assembly, pupils need to be taught (and shown how to appreciate) the qualities that will facilitate this development. This means that your provision of spiritual, moral, social and cultural development needs to be specific and identifiable (and made explicit in any documentation for which you have responsibility).

The Handbooks for Inspecting Schools clearly break down what inspectors will be considering when they make judgements about the attitudes, values and personal development of pupils at your school.

Thinking about how you can have an impact on this judgement should also reveal how well you contribute to this aspect of your pupils' education. Going through this process well in advance of an inspection gives you ample opportunity to ensure that you can make explicit what is implicit in the way to run your classroom and teach your pupils. Some ideas and thoughts for pondering have been included below. Once again, do not feel that you must work through them systematically (Table 5.4):

Table 5.4: Pupils' attitudes, values and personal development at school: teachers' checklist

a To what extent are your pupils keen and eager to come to school?

Do they arrive at school and come to lessons on time?

Do they have something to look forward to?

Are they fully engaged as soon as the school day begins (or before)?

Are young children happy to leave their carers/parents?

Is your school and classroom a safe place for pupils to be?

Do you develop home/school links to encourage eagerness to come to school?

Would your pupils say they were keen and eager to come to school?

b Do your pupils show an interest in school life? Are they involved in the range of activities your school provides?

Do you teach any pupils who opt out of school life?

Are there any activities that would bring such children within the full experience of school that might be offered (by you or someone else)?

Do they have motivations to become fully immersed in school life? Do they learn *about*, or learn *from*?

Do team sports capture the interest of your pupils?

Is pride in achievement something that you encourage?

Is the 'have a go' mentality encouraged?

Is creativity nurtured in each child?

Would you be interested in what is being offered in your classroom?

Would your pupils say they were interested in life at your school?

Table 5.4: *continued*

---

c   Do your pupils behave well in your lessons and around the school?
    Are they courteous and trustworthy? Do they show respect for
    property?

Are high standards expected of their behaviour?

Do you spend time discussing what your expected standards of
behaviour are? Do you revisit these expected standards frequently
throughout the year?

Are there any particular times during the day when poor behaviour is
more evident in your classroom? Might there be a reason for this? Is
this something that can be changed?

Is good behaviour modelled and reinforced? Can your pupils
distinguish between right and wrong?

Do they have the opportunity to work collaboratively and develop
skills of co-operation?

Are sanctions relied upon to ensure good behaviour, or is there a
culture of co-operation and a will to behave amongst your pupils?

Are sanctions for unacceptable, aggressive, disruptive or intimidating
behaviour adhered to unfailingly?

If pupils are reprimanded, do they know precisely why?

Do you adhere to your school's policy on behaviour management?

Do you relate incidents of poor behaviour to a pupil's parents/carers?

Do pupils have time to misbehave in your lessons?

Are pupils free to express gratitude?

Are pupils given responsibility for the care of school property?

Is courtesy and trust something that is actively and easily encouraged
in your classroom?

Are listening skills often revisited as part of the education that you
offer? Do pupils want to listen to adults?

Would your pupils say they behave well in your lessons and around
the school, that they are courteous and trustworthy and show respect
for property?

---

d   Do your pupils form constructive relationships with one another and
    with teachers and other adults?

Are pupils tolerant of each other's needs, skills and achievements?

Table 5.4: *continued*

Can different viewpoints be discussed in your classroom with maturity?

Is there mutual respect for what you and your pupils want to achieve?

Are pupils encouraged to listen to one another and to you?

Are pupils encouraged to help each other?

Is rudeness to you (and any other person) dealt with immediately?

Are visitors to your classroom treated with respect?

Is there a difference between the way pupils behave when they are with you and when you are not present? (Some surreptitious observation might be needed here if you are unsure.)

Would your pupils say they form constructive relationships with one another, and with teachers and other adults?

---

e Do your pupils work in an atmosphere free from oppressive behaviour, such as bullying, sexism and racism?

Are racist or sexist attitudes eliminated as soon as they arise?

Is there an open forum for the discussion of bullying, racism and sexism in your classroom?

Are there any unresolved incidents of racism, bullying or sexism that may be causing resentment in your classroom?

Do pupils know what actions you will take if they report that they feel bullied or under sexist or racist attack? Do they know whom they can talk to and what your school's internal procedures are for dealing with such matters?

Do you actively promote equal opportunities in your classroom, in a way that would be obvious to an observer?

Do you encourage the integration of ethnic minority groups in the way that you organise pupils in your classroom?

Are stereotypical views actively avoided and challenged in your classroom? Is there anything you can do to ensure this (for example, invite outside speakers to explode the myths of stereotyping)?

Do you think that your pupils feel they are able to work in an atmosphere free from oppressive behaviour, such as bullying, sexism and racism?

Would your pupils say they work in an atmosphere free from oppressive behaviour, such as bullying, sexism and racism?

Table 5.4: *continued*

f	Do your pupils reflect on what they do and understand the impact they have on others?

Are 'incidents' followed up to ensure that pupils feel the cause-and-effect link?

Do you encourage a sense of self-awareness?

Do you encourage pupils to understand that they do not exist in a vacuum, that there is interdependence and interconnectedness between humans? Do your pupils have a sense of community?

Do pupils discuss the impact that others' actions have on themselves and *vice versa*?

Do you explain why you are upset with certain types of behaviour, and what impact that has on you?

Are your pupils able to change their minds as a result of reflective processes?

Are your pupils happy with the silence of reflection?

Do you appreciate the role of emotion in your classroom? Do you act as an emotional coach?

Would your pupils say that they reflect on what they do and understand the impact they have on others?

g	Do your pupils respect other people's differences, particularly their feelings, values and beliefs?

Are differences celebrated in your classroom?

Are feelings talked about openly?

Are cultural traditions promoted and discussed at every opportunity in your classroom, perhaps through displays, visits, music, artwork and links with other schools (perhaps overseas)?

Are pupils aware of how others may perceive them? Can they temper their actions and words depending on the sensitivities of those they are speaking to?

Do you have an understanding of what 'spirit' means to you? How would you define 'spiritual'?

Do you have an understanding of what 'culture' means to you? How would you define it?

Would your pupils say that they respect other people's differences, particularly their feelings, values and beliefs?

Table 5.4: *continued*

h	Do your pupils show initiative? Are they willing to take responsibility?

Do pupils have the opportunity to show initiative? Can they act freely when something needs to be done?

Are pupils involved in your daily routines?

Do pupils have a say in their immediate environment? Do they have responsibilities for its upkeep and care?

Do you encourage each child to take an appropriate level of responsibility for his/her work?

Are there any other responsibilities you might pass on to pupils to assist the smooth running of your classroom?

Is there anything you could change to improve the initiative and responsibility shown by your pupils?

Do they thrive on challenges?

Are pupils offered choices (to encourage decision making) as often as possible?

Is there an expectation of work among your pupils?

Is self-reliance encouraged?

Is open-ended enquiry a feature of your teaching?

Would your pupils say that they show initiative and are willing to take responsibility?

i	Do your pupils have high levels of attendance and low levels of unauthorised absence?

Is attendance at school actively encouraged in those pupils for whom this is an issue, or is non-attendance accepted?

Are there any issues that may be affecting the attendance levels of any of your pupils, such as unresolved bullying?

'Irrespective of whether we are a believer or an agnostic, whether we believe in God or Karma, moral ethics is a code which everyone is able to pursue.' HIS HOLINESS THE DALAI LAMA

It is perhaps most problematic to ensure the spiritual development of pupils while they are in your care, probably because the concept of 'spirit' is so difficult to define and so frequently confused by its association with religion. At its most simple, spirituality is about relationships; with oneself, with others, with a higher self, and with nature. The following ideas may help, as may the opinions of a trusted colleague on the nature of spirituality in your classroom:

● Do you encourage a sense of awe and wonder in pupils, regarding their existence and what surrounds them, irrespective of religious belief?

● Do you have a sense of awe and wonder at what you are teaching?

EXAMPLE: When I was an NQT I had to teach a geography module on an integrated humanities course. My subject specialism is history – I do not even have any geography qualifications – so I had to learn everything only one step ahead of my pupils. The lessons I taught then were amongst the best I have ever taught. Learning about oceans and volcanoes was fascinating, and I will never forget being totally awe-struck by the depth of ocean trenches. I really think my amazement affected the way the children learnt. We certainly talked about it a lot and they would even stop me in the corridor to discuss the lessons.

● Are your pupils offered stimulating work that can ignite their imaginations? Work that embraces the cognitive, experiential and emotional?

● Are all aspects of human existence celebrated as welcome and valid experiences? Is it safe for pupils to express emotions such as joy, hope, grief, anger and love? Are there any ways you can nurture this through your work in the classroom, perhaps through circle time (which is becoming increasingly popular for all ages in all curriculum areas)?

● Can the drama of life be discussed in your classroom? What is the 'story' behind the concepts you are teaching?

EXAMPLE: The circle is hard at first. Some classes cannot handle it. It is about establishing ground rules for listening and respect. Some classes take to it straight away. They can see each other, talk to each other, and gradually they get to realise that when we are talking about our feelings we are all equal. Forty-six per cent of our kids have special needs, and working this way gives them a basis in their own experience.

- Can you use drama/role playing to enable pupils to 'be' someone or something different? To compare their existence with another's?
- Are pupils free to 'go with the flow'? Can they develop appropriate detachment?
- Do you know what your pupils' goals and aspirations are? Do *they* know? Do they have the opportunities to discover what those may be?
- Do your pupils 'discover' their education?
- Is there any piece of art, music or literature that can add depth to your work in the classroom, regardless of the subject you teach?
- Can the natural environment be brought into your teaching? Is a deep respect for nature and the natural world something that underpins your teaching?
- Can your pupils feel the 'passion' of what you are teaching them? Are you able to 'raise their spirits'? Do you feel 'spiritually and creatively *alive*'?
- Are pupils allowed a quiet time or period of silence when in your classroom, in order to focus, uninterrupted, on the work they are doing and 'connect' to it?
- Do you have a clear understanding of what characteristics would signify 'spiritual development' in your pupils?
- If asked, would you be able to give examples of 'spiritual development' that has taken place in your classroom?
- Do you know what aspects of the curriculum you teach lend themselves most effectively to spiritual development?

ABOUT

SPIRITUALITY IN SCHOOLS

▶ Spirituality in schools should not, indeed cannot, simply be provided through religious education. There is not a single curriculum area that can escape its potential role in nurturing spirituality in pupils beyond the textbooks. Admittedly, some subject areas will lend themselves more easily to this, particularly the humanities, social sciences and arts subjects, but if it was not for a quest-like spirit in the founders of other areas of study, they simply would not have existed as we know them today.

▶ Do not be put off by feelings that your pupils are too disenfranchised to benefit from any attention to spirit. Even small steps in this direction can have tremendously positive outcomes, and to be starved of spiritual nourishment at school is crippling indeed.

▶ The concept of spirit seems to have recaptured our imaginations right now. A big growth area in publishing at the moment is in mind, body and spirit books. Children's literature, such as Philip Pullman's *Northern Lights* and *The Subtle Knife* (most definitely a spiritual quest), and the ever-popular Harry Potter books (where good overwhelmingly triumphs over evil – so far!), are being devoured by adults and children alike. Some publishers, such as Barefoot Books, *only* publish books concerned with the spirit.

▶ In the world of developmental psychology, Howard Gardner's theory of multiple intelligence (see Further Reading for more information) is rapidly gaining respect, adding to our understanding of intelligence and its many strands, and the ever-increasing need for holism in the classroom.

▶ Spiritual awareness seems to be becoming more accessible, and is being presented to children in ever-more attractive ways; your work in the classroom can build on the spiritual development that pupils will be gaining (to a greater or lesser degree) outside school. Yet, it is less about adding to the existing content of your lessons and schemes of work, and more about ensuring that the content as it stands carries *meaning*.

'Spirituality is invisible. Never forget that.' STUART WILDE

The spiritual, moral, social and cultural development that takes place in schools is not always reported in inspection reports as thoroughly as it might be, and is perhaps the hardest area for Ofsted to crack in terms of having a positive impact. If it is a particular strength of yours as a classroom teacher, or your school's as a whole, you would be justified in making a song and dance about it! It should be remembered, though, that the *process* of spiritual, moral, social and cultural education is at least as, if not more, significant than the *outcome*.

A recent article by Mary Sokanovic and Dave Muller in the journal *Pastoral Care in Education*[4] listed the following definitions of the concepts of spirituality, drawn from research shared with teachers and inspectors (Table 5.5):

Table 5.5: Definitions of the concepts of spirituality

Awe	Mixed feelings of reverence, wonder and fear caused by something sublime
Wonder	Feelings of amazement or surprise
Vivacity	The quality of being animated, spirited and alive
Courage	A willingness to face or deal with danger, fear, pain or trouble, or to do whatever one thinks is right
Hope	A feeling that what is wanted can, and will, happen
Enthusiasm	Intense interest, zeal or fervour
Wholeness	Complete organisation of parts, unity and entirety
Loyalty	Adherence to one's own or other people's ideals
Uniqueness	Having no like or equal, being special
Inspiration	The stimulation or influence of some creative thought or action
Peace	A serene state of mind, calmness
Joy	A very glad feeling, delight, deeper than being happy
Spontaneity	Moved by a natural feeling or impulse, without constraint, effort or thought

Table 5.5 *continued*

Empathy	Emotional identification with another
Creativity	Use of one's inventive powers
Humour	The ability to appreciate or express what is funny, amusing or comical
Imagination	The act of creating mental images of what has never been experienced to form a new image
Curiosity	A desire to learn or know
Caring	To be concerned with, or interested in, someone or something in order to impart a positive effect
Openness	Receptiveness and responsiveness to the possibilities that exist
Pride	Delight or satisfaction in one's own achievements
Privacy	The quality of being alone, away from public view
Individuality	True to one's feelings or beliefs, authenticity

Schemes of work

The schemes of work from which you teach may be scrutinised by inspectors once the inspection has begun. They will want to make sure that what goes on in the lessons they observe has a place in the scheme; and that where pupils have been in terms of their learning relates to where they are going. There is no need to re-work these schemes, either as an individual teacher or as a department/section. As long as they are presented in a legible way, reflect the relevant sections of the National Curriculum and are followed by all who should follow them, all should be well.

In terms of assisting your inspectors in reporting positively, it would be a good idea to have some examples of work or lesson descriptions from particularly inspiring sections of your scheme(s) of work at hand, in the event of being questioned. Likewise, if you have any specific plans for improvement in the future, make sure that your inspector does not leave your school without being told.

Writing and re-working schemes of work takes a tremendous amount of effort and energy. The few weeks leading up to an inspection are no time to contemplate adding this task to your workload.

However, what should be done as a matter of priority is the preparation of detailed lesson plans for every lesson to be taught by you during the inspection period. This is not a hoop-jumping tip. Rather, by having this information (along with a copy of any worksheets or textbooks that you will be using) ready for inspectors to pick up as they enter your classroom you are helping to maximise the chances of an accurate judgement being made. See page 99 for a breakdown of what effective lesson plans should include.

Preparing resources

Naturally, when planning lessons that you know might be observed by an inspector, you will want to make sure that any resources that you use are going to impress. There is no problem with this, as long as it does not mean staying up all night, honing creative talents you never knew existed, or spending a fortune on props that may never see the light of day again!

Unless your pupils are either very young or very unobservant, they will quickly give it away if they are not used to lessons so well resourced. Just a few comments such as 'Miss, have you just worked out how to use clipart?', or 'Sir, are we doing this because the inspectors are here', will deflate your hopes of creating a slick impression quicker than you can say 'performance-related pay'!

When creating and preparing resources for your lessons, the following ideas may help:

1 Make sure that any lesson resources you prepare are not so out of the ordinary that pupils become suspicious!

2 Make sure that any resources you plan to use during the inspection week do not require inordinate amounts of last-minute preparation at a time when you will want to be focusing on other things.

3 If you plan to use a particular prop for a lesson, make sure that it works, has all its necessary parts, as well as a clear place in the curriculum, your scheme of work and the lesson itself. You should be able to relate your use of any resources to your expectations of pupils.

4 If you are planning to use worksheets or textbooks in lessons during the inspection week, aim to have enough copies so that if an inspector arrives to observe the lesson, s/he can easily follow what is going on.

5 Remember that inspectors will be more impressed with basic resources that clearly add value to your lessons, than flashy resources of dubious need.

6 Avoid using resources that will fundamentally change the way you teach. Stick with the familiar when there is a possibility that you will be observed.

7 Inspectors may want to look at the quality of resources you have at your disposal, such as textbooks, equipment and apparatus. This will help them to determine how well budgets are deployed throughout your school. For this reason, it is a good idea to ensure that any resource storage areas are organised so that a quick assessment can be made. Do not forget that comments in the final report, relating to the quality of resources you have to work with, may result in a boost to your department's or section's budget; thus, if, for example, you have suffered in the past from a dearth of quality books, make that known!

Preparing pupils' work

While inspectors are at your school, they will want to analyse samples of pupils' current and recent work. These samples will have been organised before the inspectors arrive, and you may be involved in their identification. Many schools are now annotating the work they present to inspectors, so that they have some input in placing the work within context. By storing this work (annotations intact) between inspections, you will be able to provide inspectors with an extremely useful tool when they come to assess change (improvement) over time.

Inspectors may also want to view work not identified in the samples, so it is a good idea to ensure that absolutely all marking is up to date and that pupils' work is ordered and organised. Perhaps warn pupils of the possibility that inspectors may want to look through their work. In this way, they can be prepared and may even want to offer their work to an inspector if they are particularly proud of it; something that most inspectors would be delighted at.

Managing paperwork

Now that all schools have been inspected at least once, and the demands for paperwork have been significantly reduced, you should not find yourself with a small forest to merge into your daily work! That said, Ofsted is aware that some schools are still insisting on over-preparing, generating reams of agendas for meetings, minutes, checklists and priority planners, among others. The expectation is that teachers will work through these with religious fervour, such that the pace at which staff achieve the goals set for them have a direct correlation with the rate at which their managers' stress levels recede!

Well, forget it! If you find yourself dealing with a mass of additional paperwork prior to an inspection, something has gone seriously wrong. Inspectors are sure to realise that staff are exhausted and that what they are witnessing is a stage-managed event, rather than the day-to-day work of the school.

It can be difficult to raise a voice of protest in such a culture, but these ideas may help:

▶ If a pattern of increasing paperwork develops in the first weeks after notice of inspection, talk to other staff members to see if their experience is the same. If it is, it might be prudent to request the opportunity to discuss with those producing the paperwork whether there are any viable alternatives. There *should* be the chance to do this, and staff concerns about the increase in paperwork must be recognised.

▶ If other staff are not affected in the same way, you may want to find out why you have been singled out for special treatment. Perhaps it is because you are particularly efficient or conscientious, or have skills (perhaps ICT) that will aid the preparation stages for others. If this is the case, you should be offered sufficient non-contact time so that the burden of additional work is spread more evenly.

▶ Keep discussions with other staff members going throughout the pre-inspection weeks. There may well be the possibility of sharing work done and avoiding the need for each staff member individually to 'invent the wheel'.

▶ For every piece of paper that arrives in your pigeon-hole, ask yourself 'does this apply to me?'; 'do I need to take action?'; 'what is the essence of this?'. Never file what can be recycled!

▶ If additional paperwork is sent your way, it can be effective to say 'I have X to do and then Y; if I were to do this task, which one should I drop?'. Even if you end up doing X, Y and whatever other new task, you have at least introduced the idea of bargaining for time.

▶ Respond to urgent tasks (these are usually visible to all).

▶ Keep any paperwork you receive that is specifically related to the inspection in a separate folder. The chances are that, when the inspection has been and gone, you will be able to refile this in your school's paper recycling bin! The documentation that will result from the inspection report, such as the school development plan, will take far higher priority.

▶ Keep any written communications you might need to have with other staff members to an absolute minimum.

It might sound belligerent to take such an approach to excess paperwork, but teachers rarely have time to fill when an inspection is not imminent, so there is no reason why this time should suddenly manifest itself when there *is* an inspection in sight! Inspections are important rites of passage for your school, but the attitude that no stone must be left unturned in the short time between notice and the inspection itself is more self-destructive than helpful, and tantamount (in many ways) to 'planned or anticipated crisis management'.

Highlighting evidence of your success

'Success consists of getting up just one more time than you fall down.'

OLIVER GOLDSMITH

There are certain characteristics of success that can be applied to just about every profession and relationship. If you can show your inspectors that you not only *have* these characteristics, but also *apply* them to the benefit of your pupils in the work that you do at school, there will be little left to concern you.

Think about ways of highlighting the following in your work, but remember (the now familiar reminder) that there is no need to work through these slavishly – their purpose is to trigger self-reflection where it may be of help (Table 5.6):

Table 5.6: Teachers' self-reflection focal points

Analytical thinking	Do you analyse cause and effect in your pupils' learning?
	Are you happy to analyse why something has worked (or not)?
Balance	Can you balance your work and home lives (i.e. is it all work and no play)?
	Can you demonstrate balance between the various aspects of your work at school?
Confidence	Do you give the impression of confidence to pupils and colleagues?
	Do you feel confident in your abilities?
Commitment/ dedication	Are you happy to work beyond the call of duty on the occasions that warrant such commitment?
	Are you concerned about eradicating poor performance?

Table 5.6 *continued*

Consistency	Can you demonstrate consistency in your relationships with pupils (particularly concerning rewards and sanction, and classroom rules and routines)?
	Are you consistent in the way that you manage your professional dialogues with colleagues?
Conviction	Do you know exactly why it is you work in the way that you do?
	Can you justify the professional decisions you have made?
Flexibility/ responsiveness	Are you happy to deviate from the planned when the need arises?
	Can you show ways in which you respond to the individual needs of your pupils?
Humour	Are you free to see the funny side of situations?
	Can you punctuate your work with light-heartedness, when appropriate?
Integrity	Do you allow your integrity to underpin all your work, no matter what circumstances present themselves to you?
	Are you able to influence and inspire others with your integrity?
Knowledge	Can you demonstrate a love of learning yourself?
	Are you able to keep up with technological developments, as well as the latest in educational thought and policy?
Motivation	Are you keen to discover fresh ideas and ways of working that may facilitate improvements in your pupils' learning?
	Can you muster enthusiasm even on the dark days of hard slog?

Table 5.6 *continued*

Organisation	Does your organisation of classes add to the quality of education you can offer?
	Is your organisation of all aspects of your job, particularly planning and assessment, such that you can whittle away blocks to learning?
Passion	Do you love your job?
	Can you convey to others the importance you attach to what, and how, you teach?
Perception	Can you anticipate the specific needs of your pupils in terms of targeted support and, for example, the eradication of bullying?
	Can your recognise patterns in the work and behaviour of your pupils?
Perseverance/ persistence	Do you insist on high standards of work and behaviour, even when it seems most unlikely to be forthcoming?
	Do you return to concepts that have not been grasped in a different manner that might achieve learning?
Reflection	Do you embrace your responsibilities to be a reflective practitioner?
	Do you use reflection to inform future teaching techniques?
Tact/ understanding	Do you adapt your interactions with pupils and staff when sympathy/empathy might be beneficial?
	When pupils' work is of a low standard, do they feel supported in their setting of goals for improvement?
Teamwork	Are you happy to support colleagues and help to minimise duplication of work?
	Do you express to pupils the nature of the team spirit needed for them to achieve success?
Vision	Do you have a clear idea of where you would like your career to take you?
	Do you embrace the shared vision for your school?

YOUR PROFESSIONAL DEVELOPMENT PORTFOLIO

❭ Many teachers now keep a professional development portfolio in which to record evidence of their work as a teacher. These are now proving invaluable at interviews, and many LEAs are strongly encouraging teachers to gather together pupils' work and any relevant documentation (perhaps relating to specific work undertaken at school or courses completed) in some form of folder or portfolio case.

❭ Taking the time to do this as you work through each academic year, and updating it as necessary, will mean that you have the perfect resource at your fingertips to highlight evidence of your success when inspectors visit your school.

❭ Offering a portfolio for an inspector to peruse adds to the evidence base that s/he has to work from when making a judgement on your effectiveness as a teacher.

❭ Aim for your portfolio to capture some of the complexities and dynamics of your work; if it reflects the breadth of what you do, you will be greatly assisting inspectors in their work, and they should be happy to take the time to examine it in detail.

Preparing your teaching/office space

Your classroom will certainly be seen by inspectors, but your office space (if you are fortunate enough to have it!) *may* be. While it is important for inspectors to see you work in your usual environment, many teachers like to make the most of their teaching/office space before the inspectors arrive. Here are some areas for consideration:

In your classroom, check that:

● Any broken furniture has been repaired or removed.

● Any graffiti that may be lingering can be removed or covered up, if necessary.

● Electrical sockets are safe.

● Windows are safe.

- Your displays are as you would like them to be, and mounted according to your school's mounting policy (if it has one).
- Your classroom base (be it a chair and bookshelves, desk or whole corner of your room) reflects what you want it to (i.e. how organised would it appear to a visitor?).
- All equipment in your room works or is clearly labelled otherwise (do you have enough chalk/board markers, paper, pens/pencils, tissues – whatever you use in your room on a daily basis, make sure you have plenty of supplies).
- All lights work.
- Your door (if you have one) is fully functioning.
- If you have organised your classroom into zones, they are clear for an outsider to identify.
- There is a place for an inspector to sit (but remember that, although you might invite them to sit in a particular place, they will need to move around the whole class in order to make the judgements they have to make. Do not expect them to sit tight wherever you place them!).
- If you have pupils' lockers or drawers in your classroom, they are tidy and organised. Might they be harbouring something unsavoury?
- If you need to alter the layout of your room during the actual inspection (for different types of lesson), is there anything that hinders this? Would anything ease this process (such as drawing up a plan of what should go where, or simply making sure that your room is as clutter-free as possible)?
- You have done everything you want to do in order to make your classroom as welcoming as possible.

EXAMPLE: Teachers in one school decided to spend just 15 minutes a day for two weeks in the pre-inspection stage focusing on their physical environment. The result, for many, was that the heightened organisation this gave them eased their day-to-day functioning and became a hard habit to break! It did not seem like an additional burden to workload, by limiting the time spent on this to just a few minutes each day.

When your room is empty, sit in different seats and see what view you have. Does anything that you may not normally see need attention? If any repairs need doing that have not already been flagged up, allow plenty of time for those to be organised. It might be an idea to have your room checked by the person in your school with responsibilities for health and safety.

Above all, ask yourself what there is in your classroom that has the sole aim of *empowering* your pupils. What is it that makes them feel proud of their work in your room? What is it that facilitates further learning?

In your office space, check that:

❭ Any documents, records and pupils' work that you might need to discuss with an inspector are close to hand and easily accessible.

❭ The impression you want to create is being created (might a sort-out be in order?).

❭ If there is room in your office space for discussions with an inspector, there are enough chairs for all to sit comfortably.

❭ Any stored resources are accessible and organised. Would it be easy for an inspector to assess the quality of the resources you have for teaching?

❭ Anything you would not want an inspector to see is removed (if only temporarily!).

Preparing pupils

Ofsted inspections have a high media profile, and for this reason, older pupils may be well aware of what is going on in their school, why it is happening, and also that a report on the quality of education being offered to them will soon be in the public domain.

In order to counter-balance this knowledge among pupils, some teachers feel the need to encourage the belief that it is the pupils that are being inspected, and not the teachers. By placing responsibility on pupils to perform well for them and for the school as a whole, it is hoped that disruption during observed lessons will be kept to a minimum.

This is probably a bad route to take; if your pupils are sufficiently 'switched on', they will realise that what you tell them is out of fear, rather than out of genuine concern for their welfare. Naturally, the work of a school is achieved through teamwork and pupils are central in that team, but the responsibility for a successful inspection does not lie in their hands.

1 Take time to talk to your pupils about the possibility of inspectors visiting their classroom. If there are any particular pupils causing you concern, discuss your worries with them well in advance. There is nothing wrong with telling a child what it is about his or her behaviour that you do not like, and aiming to develop strategies to nurture the child towards the expectations you have of him or her. Likewise, should a problem arise with a child during an observed lesson, make sure that you tell the inspector the background to the problem and what you have been doing to reach a solution. *Do not let inspectors leave your school without offering all the explanations that will enable them to reach true conclusions on your work.*

2 Sound relationships are essential, if you are to expect co-operation from pupils during an inspection (or at any time). Although most teachers do this all the time, do remember the importance of building good relationships on an ongoing basis. If your inspection falls at the start of the academic year and you have a new class of pupils to get to know, this task is going to be more important (and in some ways more difficult) than usual.

3 Discuss with pupils in advance of an inspection where a visiting inspector might sit in your classroom. Be prepared for the inspector to move around the classroom.

4 Explain to pupils that inspectors like to talk to children to find out what it is they are learning. This is a good opportunity to re-emphasise the standards that you expect in the way your pupils respond to visitors. Also, explain that inspectors may want to make notes of what pupils say, and that you expect them to answer all questions posed to them with honesty.

5 Some pupils may feel inhibited during class discussions if there is a stranger in the room. Explain in advance that it is safe for them to participate in discussions while inspectors are in the room, and that they should observe your usual classroom rules of respect in terms of dominating the conversation and listening to the views of others.

EXAMPLE: I had the registered inspector observing one of my year 10 classes. It was always tough-going with them, and I had been dreading one boy in particular turning up (he often did not). Well, not only did this boy arrive for the lesson on time, but also he sat right in front. His behaviour was impeccable (very rare) and he had an answer for every question I asked. I was delighted at this new-found interest in my subject, and encouraged it as much as I could. Whatever had happened, it now meant that he had sat down for an entire lesson for the first time ever! As he left the room at the end of the lesson, he winked at me and said that he had not wanted to let me down. After all our battles I finally felt we had got somewhere. The downside was that I was criticised for allowing one pupil to dominate the discussion!

6 Take this opportunity to re-emphasise respect for each other and respect for property.

7 Explain that a successful inspection is a good thing for pupils and the school as a whole.

8 Stage-managing your pupils during an inspection is probably not going to send them positive messages about the way in which you view the evaluation of your work.

EXAMPLE: There was a complete change of attitude in our school when it was inspected. When the Ofsted people left, we could actually let our shirts out, or speak informally to one another and the teachers. They had assemblies dedicated to how we should act, and if we were not to do so there would be penalties. So, what is the point of Ofsted reports, if there isn't a fair representation of the school?

1 This report is available to download from
www.dfee.gov.uk/teachingreforms/docs/hay.doc

2 *The Handbooks for Inspecting Schools,* TSO, 1999.

3 This summary can be found in *The Handbooks for Inspecting Schools,* TSO, 1999.

4 Volume 17, Number 1, March 1999. *Pastoral Care in Education* is the journal of the National Association for Pastoral Care in Education.

CHAPTER 6

Effects of inspection on the individual
Awareness and self-help techniques

'The deepest principle of human nature is the craving to be appreciated.' WILLIAM JAMES

Best and worst case scenarios

When you are facing an inspection, whether or not for the first time, it is worth taking a few minutes to analyse how you are thinking about the impending event. If there is any flicker of trepidation or anxiety in your emotions, it would be a good idea to write down what the best and worst scenarios for the inspection are. In this way, you will be in a position to dismantle the negative and extract the fear that it holds, and then focus on the positive. When teachers have done this in the past, similar themes appear to occur.

Best scenarios feature the following characteristics (among others):

- Plenty of time to plan lessons that are sure to impress;
- Impeccably behaved pupils;
- Minimum disruption to lessons and pupils;
- Inspectors with the time and inclination to hear what teachers want to convey;
- Specific recognition for contributions to the quality of education offered by the school;
- A glowing report;

- A pervading sense of calm serenity among staff;
- A great big pat on the back from senior managers!

> EXAMPLE : One secondary teacher described how, at the end of her school's inspection, staff were on an exhausted high. There had been no 'disasters' and the inspectors seemed genuinely pleased with what they had seen. As far as she knew, no teachers were particularly upset by the whole process. However, when the headteacher addressed staff at their after-inspection staffroom party, he made it clear that there was 'still much to be done' and that he wanted to see them 'bright-eyed and raring to go' first thing on Monday morning. With no 'well done, take a well earned rest' or similar, the fragile high that staff had achieved was pulled down to a crushing low in one swift tug.

Often, it is not the best scenarios that cause the most concern, although identifying them may help you to see how optimistically you are facing the inspection. If all you can conjure up as a best scenario is teaching an observed lesson where no pupils swear at you and a teaching grade that does not signify serious weakness, then you just might need a gentle nudge towards a more positive vista!

If you can envisage some worst scenarios, it is important to take a good look at them to determine whether they are *realistic* or *probable*. In most cases they are not, and should be forever banished under the heading 'temporary anxiety'. However, the following fears seem to feature fairly frequently amongst those soon-to-be-inspected.

Not having enough time to complete detailed lesson planning for the week

In the drive to get everything else done, the most important pre-inspection preparation can get squeezed. Obviously, some of the finer details of your planning will have to be done at the last minute, as it is difficult to predict precisely what work pupils will be doing in six to ten weeks time, but do make sure that you ring-fence time to focus on this. A detailed lesson plan for every lesson to be taught during the inspection week, which has a clear place in the curriculum and your scheme of work, will be invaluable in impressing inspectors. The only way to avoid this worst scenario is to plan time to plan!

Having unreasonable expectations of staff

It would be wrong not to acknowledge that, in some schools, unreasonable expectations are made of staff, and calls for assistance are seen as something negative rather than opportunities for development. Such a culture places (often unspoken) threats about chances of future promotion on staff members who deviate from compliance. Difficult as this may seem, to comply with unreasonable requests/ demands without seeking help will certainly see you in no fit state to accept a promotion, should one ever be offered! Talk to external advisors, such as Teacherline or your union, if you are likely to receive a hostile reception to any internal calls for help.

There is also a lot to be said for discussing your concerns with your leaders and colleagues face-to-face, with the intention of reaching a solution that does not involve an increased workload for you. Aim to hold any such discussions before you take on the additional expectations – if you begin and then find it is all too much, it will be far harder to negotiate assistance. The key is to be realistic yet positive about your capabilities at this time.

Not being able to manage the behaviour of pupils in an observed lesson

Even teachers who rarely experience indiscipline and non-compliance in their classrooms have expressed this concern prior to an inspection, and it is a natural concern. Behaviour management is central to your work, and many teachers achieve this through sheer force of character and personality. Therefore, it is easy to view any judgements made on your behaviour management skills as a reflection of perhaps the very essence that is 'you'. This carries a whole lot more weight for many teachers, than judgements made on other skills, hence the vicious cycle of anxiety.

If it is any consolation, most teachers report that pupils behave better than usual when an inspector is observing the lesson. In addition to this, any indiscipline, however minor, is an opportunity to show an inspector how you reinforce expected standards of behaviour and how you handle the miscreant at the time. Do not worry about this fear. Even if a lesson is a 'disaster' (rare in Ofsted's experience), development needs will be flagged up and support should be forthcoming in the near future. Affirm that behaviour in your classes will be excellent.

'Corpsing' in front of an inspector

Be realistic! Have you ever done this? What would happen if you did? Could you get out of such a situation with a '*Sorry I have lost my thread.*

Where were we? Would anyone like to help me out? Remember to put your hands up'? Inspectors are human and will be far more interested in how you deal with such an event than the fact that you corpsed in the first place. Remember that there is no such thing as the 'perfect' teacher – you are human, not an automaton!

Showing gaps in knowledge in front of an inspector

Although you will have prepared your lessons in fine detail, you can never know exactly what will arise during each lesson. There may well be questions from pupils that you are not entirely sure about, but again, remember that there is no such thing as the perfect, all-knowing teacher, and your inspector should appreciate this. Once again, how you deal with this situation will be of greater interest than the fact that it has arisen at all. More often than not, honesty is the best policy. It is far better to admit what you do not know, than attempt to bluff and risk digging a deep grave for yourself.

As long as you arrange a time when you will be able to get back to the class/pupil with the correct answer there is nothing wrong with saying something like '*I am not entirely sure of the answer to that. I will double-check and send a note via your register*', or some similar arrangement. The next time you teach that particular subject to the class, recap on the question and tell your inspector what you intend to do. You may want to invite him or her back to watch you make amends.

Not being observed for your better lessons

If you know that some particularly interesting work will be done in a lesson, or you have a visiting speaker and would like it if your inspector witnessed what happens, there is nothing wrong with inviting him or her in to the lesson. If you think that something is going to be good, do not let inspectors miss it. In most cases, if they can fit the extra observation into their schedule they will, but even if they cannot, you will have shown yourself to be embracing the spirit of the inspection and actively participating in the process, rather than being a passive recipient, and that is sure to go down well.

Facing observations for many hours each day

This has been the experience of some teachers in the past, with occasionally up to three or four inspectors in the room at the same time. Now that the framework for inspection has been refined, Ofsted's quality guarantee to teachers states that '*normally, teachers will be observed teaching for no more than half of any one day and never more than three-quarters*', but also that '*inspectors will not judge teaching unless they have observed a significant part of the lesson, normally for at least 30 minutes*'.

If the number of observations you receive becomes a source of stress for you, and you seem to be receiving more visits from inspectors than your colleagues are, speak to your headteacher who will be able to raise the issue with the registered inspector during one of their daily 'chats'. However, do keep in mind that it is far better to receive a judgement based on detailed and frequent observations of your work, than on few observations and perhaps not even of whole lessons.

Not having the opportunity to discuss work with inspectors

Your inspectors should offer you the opportunity to discuss your work with them. This 'discussion' must be two-way, as opposed to your simply answering the questions that the inspector asks. It is perfectly acceptable to influence the agenda in this way. If you are not offered this opportunity, the registered inspector should be told and every effort made to ensure that you are given time to address your concerns with inspectors before they leave your school (preferably not on the final day).

Should this not be the case, you would have cause to raise a complaint and this would normally be done through your headteacher (see Chapter 4). Do not slip into acceptance of such a situation, and make sure that you retain a written record of every attempt you have made to resolve the situation, in case it becomes necessary to make a complaint of a more formal nature.

Being misunderstood or misrepresented

The chances of this happening should be remote, but nevertheless some teachers have had this experience. If this happens during a verbal debriefing, when the inspectors are still in your school, the best way of dealing with it is to raise your concerns with your headteacher who will be able to discuss the matter with the registered inspector. Once again, it is important to keep written records of any discussions you have with either your headteacher or inspectors regarding what you consider to be a misrepresentation or misunderstanding.

If this does not resolve the situation, it may be necessary to take the matter further (see page 92), and you will be greatly assisted in this if you have the support of your headteacher. If support does not appear to be forthcoming, do get advice from your union (or several unions). Do not, however, let the situation drop if it is one that troubles you. It may seem like hassle to correct what has happened, but is vitally important for your self-esteem and morale.

Having to restructure work schemes and policy documents as a result of the inspection

Before an inspection, this should not happen under any circumstances. Ofsted's Quality Assurance Guarantee states that '*inspectors will not expect you to create additional paperwork specifically for the inspection*'. Your union should be told if you are directed otherwise by your headteacher, and if inspectors themselves have requested additional paperwork your headteacher will be taking the issue up with Ofsted and the inspection contractors.

Once the inspection has been and gone, there will undoubtedly be work generated as a result, but this should be carefully managed and contained within your school's development plan, with time scales and review dates built into the framework. Under no circumstances should you be placed under undue pressure to produce new policy documents and schemes of work. All such development should be carefully planned over a suitable period of time.

Receiving a lower than expected grade for teaching

If internal peer observations and self-observations are successful in your school, you should not be labouring under any misconceptions about your abilities and performance. Ofsted inspections should not be a source of surprise for schools. Some teachers have been disappointed with the conclusion drawn on their teaching, and this is more to do with language than anything else. There are clear definitions for each grade on the seven-point scale against which teachers are judged (see page 84).

If you still feel that you have been placed too low on the scale, you can ask your headteacher for the evidence used in reaching this decision. If, following discussions with your headteacher (and possibly other colleagues who know your work well), you collectively feel that something is amiss, your headteacher should take the matter up with the registered inspector. It may be possible for some negotiations to take place before the final report is published. If it is any consolation, recent research by Market and Opinion Research International (MORI) showed that few teachers felt that the grade they received for their teaching was important. Banish this worst scenario by appreciating that there are ways of dealing with this situation, should it arise. However, this is relatively unlikely.

Being criticised unfairly

A common complaint of many a pupil, too! Perhaps it is human nature, but it seems that teachers rarely feel they have been criticised unfairly when they are given a verbal debriefing. Problems seem to arise in teachers who feel unfairly criticised when the verbal debriefing is translated into the written report.

When you have received your debriefing, it is a good idea to make notes on what has been said, remembering the positive and the negative with equal accuracy. This will then be extremely useful when discussing your concerns with your headteacher who should take up the matter from there. If the unfairness is spoken, do not feel that you have no right to request evidence and examples. This is part of taking an active part in the inspection process, and inspectors should be happy to take part in such discussions. If they are not, you would certainly have cause for complaint.

View your inspection with optimism and determination. Pessimism cannot serve you well and will ultimately block your thinking about what it is in your job that you do really well, what you enjoy about your job, and what you are looking forward to sharing with inspectors. There are no intractable problems when it comes to inspection!

Facing criticism

'Criticism is hard to take, particularly from a relative, a friend, an acquaintance or a stranger.' FRANKLIN P. JONES

For some teachers, their accepted view of Ofsted is that it is a 'fault-finding' exercise, which makes the process of receiving any criticism even more problematic than it might be. By cringing at the thought of facing criticism, those teachers are shattering the chances of the whole inspection exercise offering the opportunity to participate in teaching actively, as a mature professional.

We cannot avoid criticism altogether, but that does not mean that you will receive more criticism than praise when the inspectors come to call. If inspectors have cause to criticise any aspect of your work or that of your school, it would be helpful to believe that this criticism is concerned and constructive, as opposed to casual and confrontational.

Much of the advice on receiving criticism suggests that taking it with friendliness and goodwill encourages positivity in the critic. If you believe that a critic has your best interests at heart, you are unlikely to respond to criticism defensively. With objectivity, you are in a position to analyse what the reasons behind the criticism might be, and whether there is truth in what has been said. In the extremely unlikely event that you can find no truth in what has been said as a result of an inspection, you need to discuss the situation with colleagues and your headteacher.

The main bonus of receiving criticism, either as an individual or as a school, is that you will not be banished to problem-solve in isolation. Negative feedback for any member of a school's community is a signal that positive solutions must be sought with support at the heart of it. Such support is usually most effective if it is not only vertical, but also lateral.

There is no doubt that receiving feedback is an essential part of our professional development, and to receive no feedback is as difficult (if not more so) than receiving negative feedback. If we analyse our working lives, we receive feedback all the time, from our everyday interactions with colleagues, from managers/leaders and subordinates, from pupils and parents, even from our own bodies and minds in terms of how we are coping with the pressures we face. Feedback and criticism should not be an exceptional aspect of working life; indeed, there would be little point in participating in a profession such

ABOUT

HIGH EXPECTATIONS

'There is no heavier burden than a great potential.'   Charlie Brown

❯ Being the 'golden' girl or boy on a team of staff can be the cause of great anxiety when an inspection looms. What if inspectors do not carry the same views? What if the dynamics in your school are altered as a result of the inspection? What if you go to pieces?

❯ Great expectations can be burdensome, but worrying about them will not ease your path through the weeks ahead. If inspectors have different views from those of your leaders and managers, perhaps there are some issues that need to be addressed (although unpleasant surprises are not a common feature of inspections); and there is no doubt that the inspection will alter the dynamics in your school to some extent. Whether or not you go to pieces is in your hands, but one thing is (almost) certain: if you do go to pieces, you will not fall apart!

as teaching if there was no opportunity for development through feedback and criticism. It might be hard to relish the thought of someone sitting in on your lessons and then offering feedback that may not be 100 per cent positive, but surely it is preferable to be given constructive, mindful feedback (assuming that is what it is) than blind, possibly ruinous praise.

> *'Nothing would be done at all if a man waited until he could do it so well that no-one could find fault with it.'* CARDINAL NEWMAN

Managing stress

> *'Within you there is a stillness and sanctuary to which you can retreat and be yourself.'* HERMANN HESSE

Recent research undertaken on behalf of Teacherline[1] has shown that:

- Over 100,000 teachers have experienced stress problematically as a result of Ofsted inspections.
- Over 50,000 teachers have experienced stress symptoms of a more serious nature during or after inspections.
- Ofsted inspections were cited as the main cause of stress in 8 per cent of all calls where stress is an issue.

A common belief among callers to the line is that teachers 'can, and should, be able to cope with anything', with comments such as 'everyone seems to be coping except me' being very common. Well, teachers do not need a book such as this to tell them that this is utter nonsense! There is nothing wrong with *thinking* that others may be coping better than you, but just know that it is highly unlikely to be true and that such thoughts do not serve you well in the long run. Encouraging open discussions about experiences of stress in your school will help you to appreciate that, while appearances may indicate otherwise, if you are feeling the effects of stress the chances are your colleagues are, too.

There is nothing unusual about stress *per se*. It can be the trigger we need to take appropriate action to drive us onwards and upwards.

However, negative stress can take its toll and lead to life threatening conditions.

Recognising the symptoms of negative stress is a major step towards eliminating its negative effects. However, it is difficult to identify exactly what symptoms can be attributed to negative stress, simply because of the fact that they may be physical, emotional, or behavioural . If you think you may be suffering from negative stress, consider these questions:

- What do others say about you? How are you described?
- How do you interact with others? Are you patient and attentive, or snappy and distracted?
- Are you less confident than you used to be? More shy and introspective?
- Is your mood stable and balanced, or do you find yourself swinging from contentment to distress in one go?
- Is decision making more difficult than it used to be and concentration a thing of the past? Do you procrastinate?
- Are your thoughts generally positive or negative? Do you have any thoughts of impending doom?
- Do you rely on stimulants more than usual? Has the occasional drink become a daily necessity? Are you comfort eating?
- Has work taken over where leisure once reigned? Once you have completed your work, do you have the energy for a full social life?
- What are your energy levels like? Do you experience the highs and lows of adrenaline 'dependence'?

ACTION: Think about how stress has affected you in the weeks leading up to your inspection. Do any problems seem to be intractable? Is there anything that you have been struggling with alone that could be easier to manage with the help of another? Write down three steps you can take towards easing the stress that you feel.

WAYS IN WHICH SCHOOLS HELP THEMSELVES THROUGH STRESS

Many schools are now devising ways in which to relieve the stress felt by teachers at inspection time. The following methods seem to be particularly effective:

> Written material on methods of stress busting within the context of the school.

> Ongoing discussions on the impact of work on the stress felt by teachers.

> Organised peer support groups.

> Confidential counselling services.

> Visiting therapists with expertise in stress reduction, such as reflexologists, yoga instructors, meditation/relaxation instructors, etc.

> Active maintenance of a collective sense of humour.

> Regular appreciation from senior members of staff.

In schools that actively seek to address the stress felt by teachers, there is an understanding that, regardless of which teachers are suffering from stress, the impact can potentially affect everyone; i.e. there is a holistic approach to the issue.

There are a number of stress warning signs to watch out for. It may be time to take positive action if you find that you are suffering from any of the following signs in Table 6.1 overleaf:

Stress busting skills

'In the depths of Winter, I finally learned that within me there lay an invincible Summer.' ALBERT CAMUS

Life does seem to have changed. This point has been made before, but it is worth emphasising again: 50 years ago, it was only bridges that were stressed! We have had to develop resilience to life stressors such as

Table 6.1: Physical and mental/emotional stress: warning signs

Physical signs

Vague feelings of ill-health
Headaches
Palpitations
Dry mouth due to decreased saliva production
Fatigue
Chemical dependence
Digestive problems
Menstrual disturbances
Weight loss/gain (most commonly loss)
Skin problems such as acne and eczema
Raised blood pressure and heart rate
Increased susceptibility to colds/'flu
Increased sweating
Grinding teeth
Shallow, rapid breathing
Tension in legs and arms

Mental/emotional signs

Memory problems
Noise sensitivity
Lack of joy/frequent crying/emotional outbursts
Hopelessness and helplessness
Depression
Preoccupation, perhaps with worrying thoughts
Inability to control anger
Difficulty in being alone
Nightmares
Feelings of dissatisfaction in personal work performance
Loss of confidence and self-esteem
Irritability

work, so that when the major events strike (such as births, deaths and marriages) we have some source of energy upon which to draw. These ideas are known to be useful for stress busting:

● Mind/body techniques such as visualisation, meditation, relaxation, T'ai Chi, yoga, etc. are known to impact negative stress. The best way of

ABOUT

DEPRESSION AND SUICIDE

❯ Stress, anxiety and depression can be extremely closely linked, and concern about their relationship with suicide is growing. It is generally understood that prolonged negative stress can contribute to mental illness and even psychiatric injury, which can lead to a heightened potential for suicide in susceptible people. One particularly vulnerable group is those teachers in their twenties or thirties who have a limited social circle (due to work commitments) and perhaps no close family around them to give a sense of perspective.

❯ If you feel that you are experiencing depressive thoughts or even contemplations of suicide, do everything in your power to muster the strength to talk to someone about how you are feeling. As soon as you have divulged even a little of the immense emotion inside, you will create the space to start thinking creatively of solutions. This, however, should not be attempted alone. There are always people with the expertise to help you – you are not alone.

❯ If you are not happy about talking to family or friends (this can be the case), then call the Samaritans (0345 909090 – emergency line, 08457 909192 – textphone) or Teacherline (08000 562 561).

❯ Make an appointment to see your healthcare provider and take someone with you if that would help you to express fully the way you are feeling. It would also be a good idea to warn those closest to you that you would appreciate it if they 'kept an eye on you'. There are always answers; you do not need to suffer alone indefinitely, but you do need to verbalise your feelings to someone in a position to facilitate hope and help.

learning such techniques is to join a class (your local sports/leisure centre or adult education centre will almost certainly run such courses). However, this might not be practical if your stress has shown itself at such a busy time! If you feel unable to join a class, try one of the excellent books that exist on this subject (see Further Reading). It is sometimes best to join such a class when your need for positive results is less urgent, because then you are free to learn what it can offer you and apply the skills on a daily basis, but especially when your stress levels rise.

● Develop and nurture a hobby, preferably a creative or sporty one. Once again, if you invest the time in this when you are not particularly stressed, you will be more likely to maintain the habit (and reap the rewards) when stress strikes.

'A hobby puts to work those unused talents which might otherwise become restless, and it provides us with a form of activity in which there is no need whatever to strive for success.' HAL FALVEY

● If you can feel stress rising, stop. Take deep breaths and ask yourself why this is happening. Be specific. What, exactly, was the trigger? What can you do about this? Go for creative, solution-driven approaches to your stress.

● Become self-observant. When you feel stressed, what are the changes that take place in your body and mind? How positive is your self-talk? Learn to recognise these symptoms as messages from your body. If your back starts to ache when stress takes hold, take action at the first twinge

ABOUT

USING AFFIRMATIONS

An affirmation is an often-repeated phrase which focuses on something positive. This is an excellent way of managing negativity, but there are some important points to remember when constructing them:

❯ Always use positive statements. Say 'My lessons that are observed by inspectors go brilliantly', rather than 'There are no problems in the lessons I teach'.

❯ Use present rather than future statements: 'The inspection is going very well', rather than 'The inspection will go well'.

❯ Visualise your ideal scenario when you use affirmations. Believe that you can create the situations you want to create.

❯ Repeat your affirmations often throughout the day.

– and better still, anticipate what makes the twinges start and take action before the symptoms have the chance to express themselves. Remember that physical symptoms are often your body's final shout that it is not happy with what you are putting it through. If you quieten your mind, you will be able to hear its pleas when it is still whispering!

● Find out what soothes you (a book, particular food, exercise, certain person or form of relaxation, etc.).

● Be watchful of those around you. Is anyone dragging you down with his or her persistent negativity? Avoid them as much as possible (unless you want to help them see more positive vistas!).

● Do not seek to attribute blame for the way you are feeling. Feeling stressed often carries with it the related notion of feeling undervalued. Of course there is a societal need to value teachers, but no one can make you *feel* valued. That is down to you, just like managing your stress can only be achieved by you.

● Take care over your diet and intake of chemicals and stimulants, such as caffeine, nicotine, alcohol and drugs. Be particularly aware of the fine line that divides social and addictive drinking. Watch out for any changes in drinking habits.

● Seek appropriate professional help as early as possible. Teacherline is a good place to start, and counsellors will be able to identify what or who would be best placed to offer you help. Recognise the resources you have inside you to take the step of seeking help.

● Do not underestimate the escapist qualities of books and music. Burying yourself in either for as little as 15 minutes can be incredibly refreshing.

● Stay in the present. Divided attention leads to tension.

Natural help for stress

Gareth Zeal, chief nutritionist of health supplement company GNC, suggests that the supplements outlined below can help to alleviate the signs of negative stress. Although there is a need to guard against 'mopping up the floor before turning off the tap', it is now thought by many that such supplements can help to enable stress sufferers to get themselves in the position of being able to seek long-term solutions to negative stress.

- Kava Kava has been shown to produce a pronounced sense of tranquillity and it aids concentration.

- Ginseng has been proven to sharpen the memory.

- Ginkgo Biloba is said to boost circulation in the brain and improve concentration.

- Magnesium levels can be depleted when the body is under strain; therefore, magnesium supplements can be helpful.

- The B vitamins will help to ensure that the nervous system can cope with the extra strain at times of stress.

- Aromatherapy can be an effective destressor. Always use aromatherapy oils diluted in a carrier oil: in a burner, or adding a few drops in a warm bath, or in massage. Ylang Ylang is good for creating a sense of peace; lavender and bergamot have sedative qualities; and Clary Sage is good for feelings of despondency and depression. See Further Reading for books on aromatherapy.

- Bach Flower Remedies can be very useful to soothe nerves, in particular Rescue Remedy.

Impact of inspection stress

'I try to take one day at a time – but sometimes several days attack me at once.' ASHLEIGH BRILLIANT

There are some clearly identifiable characteristics of the stress felt by teachers as an inspection draws near. This stress can be impacted greatly by the actions of a school's management team. Schools whose managers insist on a complete rewrite of policies, and over-emphasise the need for a glowing report, are invariably suffering under the misguided notion that the outcome of the inspection is of greater importance than the physical and mental health of staff members. These may be harsh words, but if an inspection is going to take place, the only variables are the behaviour of the inspectors and the way in which the event is perceived across the school.

Your school has total control over only one of these variables, and it can be difficult to establish a prevailing sense of realism if the expectations from above are totally unacceptable.

Dealing with pre-inspection stress must be an *enabling* process, if it is to offer teachers practical assistance within the context in which they work. These ideas may work for you:

1. Act quickly. Do not let negative stress fester until it has become so much a part of your being that all you can do is scramble out from beneath it, irretrievably affected by the impact it has had on you.

2. If you are beginning to feel stressed by the inspection, do consider the fact that it is possible to become stressed about *anything*; a visit to the dentist or even crossing the road carry inordinate amounts of stress for some people. One tried and trusted method of alleviating such stress is to bring the event down to its appropriate size in your mind. Affirm to yourself that 'it is *only* an inspection'. This can work surprisingly well. You should also consider where these feelings came from: is inspection the fulfilment of your worst fear? Why? Can you change this belief?

3. Inspection, like life, is a temporary situation.

4. Know yourself. If you can pinpoint your skills, strengths and development needs, you are unlikely to be shocked by the verdict of inspectors. If you are, it may be necessary to lodge a complaint (see page 89).

5. Focus on *your* response to the inspection, and distance yourself from the responses of others. Some people will want to push through the inspection demanding an inordinate amount of energy from themselves and those around them, while others will relax into it. Carve your own path through the pre-inspection stages.

6. Ask more questions about the inspection process. Learn about what will happen within the context of your school, so that you eliminate the chances of any shocks once the inspection has started.

7. Work as hard on your self-esteem as you do on your preparation. A solid belief in yourself will be less vulnerable than a pool of self-doubt. Throw out the 'what ifs' as soon as they enter your mind!

ACTION: The survivor traits of resiliency, flexibility and adaptability are not only crucial to happiness within the teaching profession, but to happiness in life, too. Jot down the aspects of your character that show these traits, and take a moment or two to appreciate the scope of your being. And remember – there is nothing wrong with paradoxes!

If there is one person in particular who is contributing to your stress, aim to reach an understanding of their motivations. *Why* do they find it necessary to treat you in such a way? What are *their* stressors? This in no way excuses their behaviour, but will help you to see that it is highly unlikely that the situation is personal. The only way of reaching a resolution is to talk to your stressor about what is happening. Take a trusted third person with you, if that would help (although this can be difficult to set up). Express assertively what would ease the stress you feel, and aim to reach a resolution. If you do hold such a conversation, do not let it end without moving to a more positive plain – it is possible to create win/win situations if both parties guard against identifying character flaws in the other. Document what you say in case you need to refer to it at a later date.

Expect the most positive outcomes. Feel positive about the inspection. Mentally rehearse what you want to convey to inspectors. Visualise what their responses might be and prepare replies to potential questions. Even if your visualised scenarios do not materialise, you will have mentally prepared yourself for constructive discussion with your inspectors. Many sports men and women and performers take this approach of mental rehearsal. It seems to be the case that if you are unable to see in your mind's eye a particular outcome, the chances of it happening are much diminished. Above all, act 'as if…' and cast yourself in the role of success.

Be utterly realistic in your goals. If in doubt, err on the side of caution in committing to work. Do what you must do first (keep your real priorities in sight), then what you want to do, and do not balk at the notion of negotiation. If you are asked to perform a task that will tip you over into the realms of negative stress, you are entitled to employ a little bargaining power: '*I will be able to do X if I leave Y until after the inspection. Will that be acceptable? Yes/No? So, what is your preference? X or Y?*' Become a 'broken record' if necessary (i.e. repeat your position without deviation).

ABOUT

ASSERTIVENESS

> Being assertive is not about being selfish or aggressive, but it can be a vital tool for maintaining your sanity! When asserting yourself:

> Do not expect people to know what you need. Be as explicit as possible about what you want.

> Do not feel you are burdening others. You have a right to be assertive.

> Script what you want to say in advance. Become a 'broken record' if you have to.

> Pay attention to your body language. Are you giving clues away that you do not fully believe in what you are saying?

> Be willing to negotiate.

Remember that there is no negative stress inherent in the concept of inspection. Negative stress can only occur as a result of a response to what is happening; the stimulus (inspection) is not the reaction (stress). That said, feeling stressed is not your fault, but do not feel powerless in bringing about an end to the stress.

Take a walk outside as soon as possible after feelings of negative stress begin to manifest. Even if this is only for a few minutes, a blast of fresh air can help you to shift perspective.

Give yourself permission to face your feelings of stress. If you had broken your leg, you would accept that you could not drive while it was encased in plaster – you would not give yourself a hard time over having to alter your way of being until healing had taken place. The same applies to negative stress. If a day off would help, take it. If delegating some basic chores would help, delegate. If a reduction in your workload would help, do all in your power to achieve this (use your powers of persuasion, script what you want to say, and be mindful of your body language). Whatever you do, do not add to the expectations you have of yourself; the relationship between workload and stress is well known.

Organise your workload into timed slots and be very strict about going over-time. This also applies to meetings in the pre-inspection weeks; these should have an end-time that is religiously adhered to.

ABOUT

STRESS, INSPECTIONS AND SIGNIFICANT OTHERS

▶ There is no doubt that being involved in 'special' work projects, such as an inspection, will have a knock-on effect on those you live with.

▶ Through the research for this book, several headteachers and classroom teachers made the comment that those about to undergo inspection should warn their significant others that they may be distracted by the process for a while, and that they may need more support than they can give, at least in the short term.

▶ It can be easy to exhaust the patience of those you live with, if you do not communicate why it is that you are perhaps more tense than usual or working with increased intensity. Friends, family and significant others are far more likely to offer practical assistance if they know in advance what is going on in your life and how you might be affected. There is a work/home interface that can too often become blurred to the point of being unrecognisable for many teachers.

EXAMPLE: Now I look at myself. I am not the most confident of people at the best of times. Fourteen years in the job, I know my limitations. I have not gone for promotions because I am very well aware that I am not secure enough in the paperwork area to take on more responsibility. I have had a lot of personal stress over the last 18 months with family deaths and relationship break-ups. Now I find myself with the second-worst class in the school and the prospect of the worst class during the inspection! And this has been openly acknowledged by our Head! You can see there is a certain amount of stress building here.

Take a while to analyse whether there is a way in which you are spending time which is not productive.

Review what you can drop from your 'to do' list. Make plenty of sleep a priority, and put as many non-urgent tasks/events as possible (in any aspect of your life) 'on hold' to facilitate this.

Identify the quiet times in your working day. Take the time to look out of the window for a minute or two, or sit in an empty room for a while during your lunch break. Drive to and from work in silence.

EXAMPLE: I was Primary Science Teacher of the Year a few years back. This does not prevent me from being extremely nervous when being judged by an Ofsted inspector. I have had success in a national competition and in an Ofsted inspection, and yet I would still have concerns about teaching in front of an inspector. After all, so many things can go wrong in a lesson, no matter how successfully a teacher has prepared and no matter how good s/he is. This is because we are not perfect and when we are nervous things do not always go as planned, and we can forget important points. I think the key here is to keep a sense of humour and keep talking to each other.

Watch your movements; aim to walk more slowly and be conscious of stilling your mind regularly.

Book yourself a day of doing nothing towards your job or the inspection (and that means absolutely nothing!).

Bullying-induced stress

It seems to be the case that it is not just pupils that suffer from bullying in schools. While it would be considered an omission of a school not to have a policy for dealing with child-on-child bullying, the number of schools that have clear guidelines for the eradication of staff bullying remain few and far-between. Bullying and stress are closely interrelated, so if you are suffering from workplace stress it is essential to determine whether or not bullying may be the cause.

While everyone has a clear understanding of the kinds of behaviour that constitute bullying between children, there is no clear consensus on what adult-on-adult bullying really is. Within the context of a school (especially one approaching inspection), it would be reasonable to define bullying as:

- insidious, relentless criticism (without the offer of constructive, corrective advice);
- humiliation (such as reprimands in front of other staff or pupils);
- excessive work expectations (unrealistic demands prior to an inspection);
- abuse of discipline and competence procedures;
- inappropriate forms of communication (shouting, ordering, or 'death by a thousand memos');
- inexcusable blocks to vital information;
- the withholding of recognition for performance;
- manipulation;
- lack of compensation for difficult circumstances.

The impact that this bullying can have is likely to be significant. Sufferers may find themselves having to contend with:

- reactive depression;
- hyper-vigilance;
- shattered confidence;

– anxiety;

– fatigue;

– stress;

– digestive disorders;

– menstrual disorders.

All perfectly normal under the circumstances, but these symptoms should be short-lived, provided that the source of the bullying is dealt with.

ABOUT

ADULT BULLIES

An adult bully seeks to exert power negatively and consistently over another person, with the purpose of inciting fear and causing professional and emotional damage. There is inherent destructiveness in the bully, but it should be remembered that his/her actions often result from feelings of inadequacy which are deflected onto another person who may be accused of displaying the very flaws that the bully fears are evident in himself or herself.

Just as children are often bullied for positive traits, the same can be true of adult victims who may be seen as being too popular, accomplished, incorruptible or highlighting incompetence through their competence.

There is a clear difference between strong management and bullying. Good managers will have systems in place to detect aspects of the work performance of colleagues that may need correcting and give advice in good time. This is a crucial part of their job. Yet, there are tell-tale signs of bullying-tolerant institutions, indicating that the line between strong management and bullying is frequently crossed. These signs include high absenteeism and turnover of staff, low morale amongst staff, and a sub-culture of disrespect of management.

Vertical bullying (manager on subordinate) usually occurs before an inspection, if the management team/head is concerned about known areas for development that have not been adequately addressed. Fear is often at the root of such reactions, but knowing this does not excuse the bullying. If you fall victim to those around you who are trying to cover themselves, you need to take action.

Do remember that workplace bullying is illegal on several grounds, and the responsibility for its prevention lies firmly with your employers.

If you find yourself dealing with pre-inspection bullying, this action plan may help:

1 Talk to a trusted friend about your experiences. Second opinions can help to re-establish perspective, and may help you decide whether or not to take action.

2 Re-read your job description and any other information on teacher responsibility, such as *The Burgundy Book*, which should be available for inspection at your school's office.

3 Read about assertiveness, or attend an assertiveness course. If your professionalism is under question, you will need to be able to deal with the situation rationally and calmly. Professional counselling would also be a good idea. Contact your local education authority or Teacherline for more information. Difficult as this may seem, try as much as possible to avoid allowing the situation to permeate every aspect of your life.

4 Seek advice from Redress: The Bullied Teachers' Support Network (see below) and your union.

5 Bullying destroys good teaching, and you do not want to be facing accusations of incompetence prior to an inspection as well as the bullying itself. Most unions have their own guidelines on dealing with bullies at work, available to members and non-members (although you may have to pay for literature from unions that you do not belong to).

6 Ask for a copy of your school's policy on workplace bullying.

7 Read about workplace bullying. There is a growing number of books on this subject (see Further Reading) and these will serve to reassure you that you are not alone, as well as offer practical suggestions for solutions.

8 Speak to colleagues about what is happening to you. You may find that others are suffering, too.

9 Document all communication you have with your bully – even relatively informal contacts. If you need to refer to previous conversations this will serve you well, and so it should not be viewed as unnecessarily paranoid behaviour.

10 Refute all unfair claims that are made against you – in writing if necessary – and keep records of anything you say or write.

11 Monitor any changes in your work performance due to bullying.

12 Visit your GP, even if your health does not appear to be suffering. It is sensible to have formally recorded what is happening to you and whom you consider to be responsible. Your GP should be able to offer stress-busting advice and will be a source of support, should you need to take time off school. You should record any instances of ill health resulting from bullying in your school's accident/incident book.

There are several sources of help for the bullied teacher, both internally and externally. Internal support may come from:

- anyone who is not your bully;
- your union representative;
- the person with responsibilities for staff welfare;
- a governor who is attached to your class/department.

External support may come from:

- redress;
- your union;
- Teacherline;
- your local education authority education personnel department;
- books on dealing with bullying;
- your GP or other healthcare provider;
- family and friends.

Unfortunately, there have been cases of inspection being used as a tool for bullying. Some teachers have feared (whether rightly or wrongly) that their headteacher has 'poisoned' the registered inspector's mind with tales of incompetence and criticism. It is worth remembering that this is unusual. In doing such a thing, a headteacher is admitting incompetence of his or her own, which should be transparent to a registered inspector! Inspectors should not make judgements about your performance without observing your teaching and talking to you about your work. These are your opportunities to convey an accurate sense of your abilities and should override any opinions that inspectors may have been fed.

If you feel that you are a victim of such underhandedness, you should seek help from Redress and your union as soon as possible. This is a most serious situation that needs swift, professional handling. It may also be necessary to lodge a complaint with Ofsted.

ABOUT

REDRESS

▶ Redress is an organisation that has been set up to offer advice to teachers who feel they may be suffering from workplace bullying. It offers many forms of support and aims for fast, effective intervention in order to bring an end to the bullying.

▶ The success of Redress can be attributed to many factors. With the consent of the sufferer, Redress may make public their situation before it escalates, or inform the governors or senior management of a school about what is happening. The organisation realises that the umbrella of confidentiality can sometimes hide a multitude of sins, including professional misconduct, and seeks to stop this from happening.

▶ Redress also uses the services of lawyers who are expert in both employment and education law. Do, however, contact Redress sooner, rather than later.

Focus on anxiety

'Happy the man who has broken the chains which hurt the mind, and has given up worrying once and for all.' OVID

There comes a point when excess negative stress can develop into a full-blown anxiety disorder. Concern about the forthcoming inspection may escalate until anxiety inhibits normal functioning. This in turn leads to an increase in stress, and so the cycle is perpetuated. Although this is relatively rare (there is some evidence for a genetic predisposition), and most teachers do not develop anxiety disorders, it is very important to know what the warning signs may be. If this is an issue for you, seek the help of your chosen healthcare provider before the situation deteriorates, especially because what some sufferers believe to be anxiety may in fact be depression.

We do not have that much control over the arrival of fear and anxiety as emotions. Fear certainly has its uses as it can protect us from danger, but when it becomes subjective, problems can arise. Fear and anxiety before an inspection, by definition, are subjective. No one can know in advance what the dynamics between your team and your school will be, nor what the outcome of the inspection will be. There has to be an element of 'taking the plunge' and going forward into the inspection with determination, such that anxiety about the unknown does not control your response to the situation.

Do keep in mind that fear and anxiety in response to an inspection are more likely if you are suspicious of the procedures and what might happen.

There is nothing strange about self-doubt. What professional has not experienced some element of self-doubt at some stage? Indeed, it can even lead to an increased drive for improvement in performance. If this self-doubt becomes excessive, or out of proportion, or if it begins to paralyse you, expert help is needed. Go into an inspection with the knowledge that you cannot lose. If you are praised highly, allow yourself to feel satisfaction and fulfilment in your work. If you are criticised, or if development needs are highlighted, move towards the necessary improvements (or lodge a complaint, if appropriate) and allow yourself to feel satisfaction and fulfilment in your work. Take *neither* on board indefinitely.

There are both physical and mental symptoms of anxiety to watch out for.

Symptoms

The following may be felt to greater or lesser degrees (Table 6.2):

Table 6.2: Physical and mental/emotional anxiety: warning signs

Physical signs

Racing heartbeat
Breathing difficulties/ hyperventilation
Dizziness/light-headedness
Nausea
Increased/excessive sweating
Temperature fluctuations
Pins and needles
Menstrual and digestive disorders
Restlessness
Fatigue
Insomnia
Muscle tension

Mental/emotional signs

Diminishing concentration
Terror or a feeling of impending doom
Fear of losing control or sanity
Loss of self-esteem
Preoccupation with health
Low mood

ABOUT

DEALING WITH ANXIETY

❯ It is not always helpful to 'cope' with anxiety. By 'coping' you would be accommodating the anxiety, making room for it in your daily routines. The better aim would be to resolve the anxiety so that both physical and mental symptoms recede, helping to minimise the chances of a recurrence.

❯ Resolving anxiety can be a difficult journey as, in most cases, there will be several contributing factors at its root. That said, with the help of a trusted healthcare provider, it is not a 'mission impossible'.

When anxiety turns into panic

If the pre-inspection period at your school finds you experiencing not only stress but anxiety and panic as well, then there is an urgent need to address the causes. Several people can help you in doing this, so never feel that you are working alone.

Within your school, trusted friends on the staff may offer support, as may the person (usually a headteacher or deputy) with responsibilities for staff welfare. There is no one in your school's community that does not have someone to turn to for advice. Even headteachers can look to governors, other headteachers and the local education authority.

Outside your school, your local education authority or union may have a confidential stress counselling line, and there is always Teacherline (tel. no. 08000 562 561). Family members and friends may be a source of unparalleled support. Your healthcare provider will have seen numerous cases of anxiety and panic, and will probably have extensive experience of facilitating solutions. You will be far from alone.

If you suspect that your stress has developed into anxiety and even panic, these points may be helpful:

1 The way you are feeling is not abnormal – it is merely an exaggerated response than can be tamed.

2 As long as you address any panic you may experience, long-term harm is highly unlikely; in fact, you will probably learn more about yourself through such experiences than you had thought possible!

3 However difficult it may seem, try not to add to your panic by thinking about other things that could possibly go wrong. This can be a challenge, but in a negative state of mind it is easy to slip into thoughts of intractable doom.

4 Stay as much as you can with what is happening at the present moment, *not* what might never happen in the future.

5 Allow your panic to wash over you when it arises. This will help you to understand that it is a temporary situation that will pass. If you are at school, do all you can to get some time alone or in a quiet room, even if it is only for ten minutes. Some people with experience of panic find it is helpful to focus on something *outside* yourself as you breathe deeply to restore balance. For example, a picture, a flower, the view from a window.

6 Pay attention to your breathing. The deeper you can breathe, the faster you will return to balance. There is only so far panic can go in a body that is breathing calmly and deeply! Breathing into a hand cupped over your mouth and nose will allow you to re-breathe some of the carbon dioxide gas you have exhaled. Extend this calm to your movements; walk in a measured way and avoid the need to rush, if at all possible.

ACTION: Relax your jaw by unclenching your teeth, placing your lips lightly together and your teeth slightly apart. It is virtually impossible to retain tension in your face in this position. Then start 4-2-4-2 breathing; i.e. breathe in to a count of four, hold for two, breathe out to a count of four, and pause for two. Keep going until the panic recedes.

7 After an episode of panic, spend time focusing on everything you have achieved in the past. What is *really* blocking your success this time?

8 Once the feelings of panic have receded, complete a task that you know will be successful, however small it might be.

9 Affirm to yourself that there is plenty of time to complete all you have to complete. You could even construct a panic busting affirmation that you repeat regularly to yourself throughout the day. Anticipating work not yet done simply leads to weariness!

10 Know that, whatever your pre-inspection weeks present, you will handle it; nothing terrible will happen. In fact, your confidence and self-esteem will probably blossom!

11 Check yourself when you say or think 'what if' – a blind line of enquiry, if ever there was one!

12 If you have not enjoyed inspection in the past, do not relive those experiences in the present. What makes you think the same situations will recur? Remember that, often, what we perceive is happening and what *actually* is happening are two completely different things.

13 Regular peer observation kills fear. If anxiety has become an issue with you, get someone into your lessons quickly to help give you some perspective. Seek out colleagues who support positivity, and be mindful of the influence that others have on your approach to the inspection.

14 Treat yourself with respect. Think how you would deal with the situation if a child came to you with growing anxieties. Would you treat that child with impatience, or with compassion and concern?

So, in brief:

- Your feelings are not abnormal.
- Address your panic.
- Do not add to your panic.
- Stay in the present moment.
- Do not resist your panic.
- Pay attention to your breathing.
- Focus on your achievements.
- Complete a small, easy task.
- You *will* handle it.
- Do not say 'what if…'.

- View each inspection with fresh eyes.
- Ask for lesson observations.
- Respect yourself.

'The greater the emphasis upon perfection the further it recedes.'
HARIDAS CHAUDHURI

ABOUT

PANIC ATTACKS

❯ These episodes must be treated seriously, as experiencing a panic attack is one of the strongest signals your body can give you that negative stress has taken hold. The symptoms of a panic attack can be so severe that the sufferer may mistake them for a heart attack.

❯ Panic attacks usually include shortness of breath, palpitations, sweating, chest pain and a feeling of certain impending doom, often occurring suddenly and without warning. They are perfectly treatable, but on no account should they be ignored. If you suspect you have suffered a panic attack, seek the advice of your healthcare provider.

❯ Evidence is mounting on the success of flower remedies in overcoming panic attacks. Try Bach Rescue Remedy or Emergency Essence.

Lifestyle changes

'An optimist expects his dreams to come true; a pessimist expects his nightmares to.' LAWRENCE J. PETER

Studies have shown that people who suffer from anxiety and panic disorders are also more likely to abuse alcohol and drugs, have a greater risk of suicide attempts, spend little (if any) time on hobbies, and feel physically and emotionally weaker than others. Clearly, there are some lifestyle changes that can be adopted in order to focus on these findings, minimise the impact that anxiety can have, and help to encourage balance.

- If you smoke, seriously consider giving up.
- Keep a close eye on your alcohol intake. If an evening drink becomes *drinks* (three, four, five, etc.), or if you find yourself needing to pop out at lunchtime for a drink, you are likely to be adding significantly to the physical stress on your body. Alcohol can also worsen existing symptoms if anxiety has taken hold.
- Processed food can feed anxiety. Aim to simplify your diet with the focus on fresh fruits and vegetables, grains and pastas.
- Go easy on caffeine. It seems that people with a susceptibility to anxiety suffer the ill-effects of caffeine more profoundly than others. Watch out for hidden caffeine in chocolate, some carbonated drinks and some medicines.
- Magnesium is said to offer relaxation to those with mild anxiety. Take 200-300 mg of magnesium two to three times a day. Furthermore, anecdotal evidence suggests that soaking in a hot bathtub containing one to two cups of magnesium sulphate crystals (such as Epsom salts) for about 15 minutes can offer relief from anxiety.
- Give yourself time to pursue a hobby, however busy you may be. Even spending ten minutes a day doing something you really enjoy can be enough to give you a boost.
- Keep talking about what it is that is worrying you. Whether you talk to an anonymous counsellor on the end of a phone line, or your partner or other family members, the more you get things out in the open (and 'off your chest' – a common site of tension) the less they can fester.

Therapies that can help

Many doctors are now advocating the use of natural therapies in the drive to combat anxiety. Therapies that use touch, such as massage, acupressure and reflexology, can be extremely soothing. Herbalism and homoeopathy use natural, proven, anxiety-reducing substances that provide relief with no side-effects. Hypnotherapy and visualisation techniques help to tame unruly thoughts, as well as calming the body.

> **NOTE TO HEADTEACHERS:** *The vast majority of teachers who contributed their thoughts and ideas to this book were keen to emphasise that praise and appreciation from their headteacher were key factors in keeping stress levels down in the run-up to an inspection.*

Finding relaxation time

'You will never find time for anything. You must make it.'
CHARLES BUXTON

'For every time in stress, you need a recovering time in relaxation.'
EMMETT E MILLER MD

Teachers are creatures of habit; usually the work habit! For this reason, many teachers must make a conscious *choice* to relax. This can be even harder than usual when an inspection looms and words such as 'should', 'ought to', 'got to' or 'have to' fill the minds of the conscientious. The auto-pilot steps in, the inner voice calling for rest and relaxation is silenced, and it becomes 'heads down for a crash landing'; for that is most certainly what will happen if quality relaxation time is not pursued with the vigour that perfectionism in the classroom is.

The usual reasons for denying relaxation time are typically:

● I have to keep working because my competence depends on it;

● I have to keep working, because if I stop I will never pick up the pace again;

● If I keep working I will make things easier for myself in the future, and then I will be able to take advantage of all my hard work;

● I have to keep working because it is lazy not to – relaxation is a waste of time;

● If I am not working, I am not achieving.

In reality, all these reasons are nonsense, and it is a perversion of reality to assume that you do not need to rest, or do not have time to.

ABOUT

THE IMPORTANCE OF SLEEP

'Don't take tomorrow to bed with you.' NORMAN VINCENT PEALE

▶ One of the most common causes of insomnia is stress; yet, ironically, it is when we are under perceived stress that the restful state of unconsciousness that sleep offers is most needed. Not only does sleep refresh us for a new day, but when the body is asleep cell damage is repaired and immune function is at its most active.

▶ Increased health niggles, such as colds and coughs, seem to be an inevitable consequence of lack of sleep which in turn impacts day-to-day functioning. On top of this, when tiredness takes hold, everything seems so personal; every comment heard can feel like a put-down, and it can seem that the rational mind has gone absent without leave! So much of our well-being hinges on good quality, uninterrupted, sleep.

▶ Camomile tea before bed to ward off insomnia may be a bit of an old folk remedy, but there are many who would not be without it. Studies have shown that camomile contains compounds with calming actions.

▶ Caffeine is often consumed in greater quantities when under stress, but its adrenaline mimicking qualities lead to an increase in nervous tension, thus exacerbating the problem. Opt for caffeine-free drinks where possible, but if you have a long history of caffeine consumption do not expect to reduce consumption without withdrawal symptoms. Caffeine is addictive, so cutting back slowly is the wisest way.

▶ Take time to unwind before going to bed, even if only for 15 minutes. Working late simply borrows time from the next day. Avoid news programmes at this time (even try a 'news fast').

▶ Aim to regulate your bedtime so that your body gets into the habit of sleep. Go for more hours of sleep before midnight.

▶ Do not spend hours in bed being unable to sleep. Try getting up (but resist the urge to work), and perhaps do some light reading to bring sleep on.

▶ Always seek the advice of your chosen healthcare provider if sleeplessness becomes a habit.

Unless you allow yourself to switch off from work on a regular basis, your performance will decline and your stress levels will soar; it is as simple as that. Relaxation is not an optional extra in your life, but a vital necessity. Unless your body is able to relax, your responses to potential stressors will be far too quick, with physiological and psychological consequences.

The most effective way of ensuring that you have the time to relax on a regular basis is to *commit* to something that you find restful or relaxing. This might be some form of sport that you take part in each week, or a meditation or yoga class (with the added bonus of learning techniques that can be adopted on a daily basis). Some schools even have organised relaxation therapies that staff can choose to take advantage of before leaving at the end of the day.

If you do not have a slot in your life for 'active' relaxation, you are putting yourself at greater risk of succumbing to the ravages of unchecked stress. By investing in relaxation, your payback will be a greater ability to focus during the time you allocate to work (not to mention improved sleep quality and, in most cases, improved work and personal relationships).

Focus on health

Add an inspection to your usual working day and it is no surprise that your thoughts and actions will become geared towards it. Additional preparation is inevitable, however skilfully it is kept to a minimum by your school's managers. At such a time, it is easy to become neglectful of basic health needs.

Many schools report increased levels of sickness in the months following an inspection. It is too early to say whether this trend is continuing with the new framework for inspection, but what is clear is that some time spent focusing on health needs in the weeks leading up to an inspection may help to avoid a health crisis afterwards. Good health is not a foregone conclusion, and there are no magic recipes for its maintenance. For most people, it is a matter of ongoing self-obser-vation in order to maintain balance, remembering that prevention is a more favourable option than cure. The following ideas may appeal to you:

- Ginger has been shown to keep the brain alert. Perhaps try some lemon and ginger tea as a pick-me-up, rather than ordinary tea or coffee, if you are in need of an injection of mental energy.

- Take regular exercise, even if it is just brisk walking. It is possible to feel the benefits from as little as ten minutes of focused exercise a day, but if you can do more, all the better. Choose something you really enjoy so that you are likely to continue with it when work pressures fluctuate.

- Teaching is a high-energy profession and more physically demanding than many outside the profession can imagine. Find out what boosts your energy – perhaps a good quality multi-mineral supplement or a natural therapy treatment – and be conscious of when your energy is waning and you need a lift.

- Evidence is mounting in favour of good quality antioxidants in the battle to prevent serious illnesses such as cancer. By eliminating harmful free radicals in your body, antioxidants play an important role in the maintenance of good health.

- If fatigue is an issue for you, aim to eat at least one raw meal a day. Raw food is said to place fewer demands on the digestive system, leading to more efficient assimilation of energy. Eating small amounts regularly throughout the day (sometimes referred to as 'grazing') can also help you feel more energised, especially if your emphasis is on fresh fruit and vegetables.

- Drink plenty of water. It flushes toxins from the body like no other liquid, and is also extremely effective at keeping headaches at bay if drunk at the first sign of pain. Water is such a health-giver that headteachers would be wise to install water dispensers in every classroom, so that teachers could keep properly hydrated throughout the school day.

- If you feel that your health may be suffering as a result of the work you are doing, make a list of your duties and responsibilities that can be carried out temporarily by others. For example, if cooking is usually shared in your household, perhaps you could be given a break until you feel able to resume duties. Actively seek the help of others; you will probably be surprised at how keen friends and family members are to help out if you ask in good time.

- Take an immune system boosting supplement if you feel that you are succumbing to bugs and germs. Echinacea, garlic, bee pollen and aloe vera are good choices; your local health store will be able to identify the best one for you, or alternatively consult a qualified practitioner.

- Be mindful of your thinking. There is no doubt (as numerous studies have shown) that optimism and positivity can halt the course of illness and, indeed, help to prevent it from taking hold in the first place. If you respond well to humour, actively seek it out as often as possible; laughter is another reliable health-giver.

Your healthcare provider should check out any persistent health problems that you may have.

ABOUT

FIGHTING COLDS

A simple fact of life is that, when we are under pressure at work, our immune systems take a battering. The evidence of this is the frequency with which people succumb to the common cold. While most doctors would say that a cold lasts a week if you treat it and seven days if you do not, there are a few steps you can take that will ease your suffering and perhaps help to prevent a recurrence.

At the first sign of congestion:

❯ Take high doses of a good quality vitamin C (i.e. not a synthetic chemical version).

❯ Suck a zinc lozenge; zinc is thought to reduce the time you are sick.

❯ Eat lightly (as much raw food as possible) and drink plenty of water (at least ten glasses a day) as this helps to flush out toxins.

❯ Use eucalyptus essential oil to clear sinuses (put a couple of drops on a tissue and inhale).

❯ Take time off sooner rather than later if the cold takes hold.

Boosting morale

There is no doubt that the collective morale of a school's teachers can take a battering at the prospect of an inspection. For whatever reason, negative views of inspection can overshadow the potential benefits, and the downward spiral into resistance is more likely than the nurturing of resilience.

That said, the overall boosting of morale needs to be the responsibility of all teachers and not only of the (possibly) few to whom this is especially important.

'Lifting' colleagues

There seems to be a flourishing of what can only be described as 'inspection folklore' in many schools today. Ideas and coping strategies are being shared and successfully implemented. The following ideas have worked well in schools in the pre-inspection stages:

a   Actively seek opportunities to praise other members of staff about some aspect of their work (no matter how small). One school actually requested that each member of staff is to say three encouraging things to another staff member each day. *All* school personnel were included.

b   Never forget the positivity of humour. Laughter has an amazing ability to mellow the mind, reduce blood pressure (albeit temporarily), oxygenate the blood and thus increase energy levels, and relax muscles. Many hospitals have collections of humorous writing for patients to read; and research into the positive benefits of laughter is being published thick and fast. In Canada, it was found that managers who facilitated the best performance in employees used humour more often than those who did not.

c   Research in California has also found that laughter can strengthen the immune system. Making valid complaints to the relevant people is an essential way of encouraging improvement, but the staffroom is rarely the right place for this. Aim to relate funny incidents as frequently as possible, and remember the saying 'He who laughs, lasts'. Forget the 'inner child', this is a time for the 'inner comedian'!

d Encourage perspective in staff. A school inspection does not need to rule your happiness or self-worth. Recognise what you and others can control (such as your responses to situations) and cannot control (such as the fact that you will be inspected throughout your teaching career). Strive for balance even when emotions are running high.

e Music is a great way to ease strains and soothe minds. Either encourage the use of recorded music in your school whenever possible or, as one school did, get a live band together. You may be amazed at the hidden musical talents that colleagues have as they lull (or otherwise) away the Ofsted Blues!

f Be aware of your confidence levels before an inspection. If you feel them slipping for any reason, you may be more vulnerable to what others say. Just a few words or a look can shatter esteem at such times, and being conscious of this can prevent what at other times you may see as an overreaction. Be aware also of the impact of your words on others who may be similarly vulnerable.

g Do not break up the usual pattern of morale boosting in your school. If birthdays are normally recognised by staff, make an effort to keep that up even at the busiest of times. If there are usually staff social events, do not stop that just because of an inspection. Social events that include significant others can be especially helpful at inspection time. There is no doubt that an impending inspection has an impact on home relationships; having the opportunity for your non-teaching loved ones to talk to others about what is going on will help them understand that you really are quite normal (or not, as the case may be!).

h Treat yourself and others – no matter how small the treats are. It is amazing what impact the words 'I saw this and thought of you' can have!

i Be vigilant of the concerns of others. If another staff member confides in you their anxieties about the inspection, simply listen rather than trying to problem-solve. Give as much time as you can for the other person to talk, and try not to interject with your own thoughts and anxieties. That can be very difficult to do, especially if you share the same concerns, but is very important.

j Do remember that, for some people, sympathy is not a healer! Only when the concerns have been fully expressed should you seek to raise their positivity by suggesting (or helping them to suggest for themselves) a possible way forward, even if that is simply to talk to a different member of staff more suited to dealing with the issue. If listening to another brings up your own anxieties, do not squash them down; seek your own confidant. There is no problem with going to pieces – just don't fall apart!

k It can be easy, when facing a significant event, to lose sight of all that lies beyond. Remember, and encourage others to remember, that the inspection phase will pass.

l If morale has slipped towards the expectation of a negative experience of inspection, remind yourself and others that an open mind will serve you far better than a closed one.

m Talk to staff at all levels of the hierarchy in your school when the opportunity arises. Life for those at the top of the responsibility ladder can be lonely, stressful and isolated.

n Beware of the myths surrounding the inspection – there are some strange tales doing the rounds out there.

---

1 *Teacherline: First Report*, Patrick Nash, TBF, May 2000, available to download from **www.teacherline.org.uk**. Actual usage of Teacherline is 9.1 per cent of teachers aware of the service.

CHAPTER 7

After the inspection

Once the inspection is over, you will be a long way towards completing an important phase of your career. Although there is still work to be done (a non-specific and irritating phrase, if ever there was one), you could be forgiven for wanting to breathe a big sigh of relief.

Post-inspection stages

Although brief feedback will probably have been offered to your headteacher when the inspection drew to a close on the final day, your registered inspector will also hold a team meeting once all the first-hand evidence has been collected and considered. The purpose of this meeting is to reach corporate judgements that reflect the views of every inspector on the team.

Before these corporate judgements are written up in a formal report, your registered inspector will discuss the findings with your headteacher (who may invite any members of staff to be present at the meeting). Your governing body will also be offered the opportunity to talk about the findings. The emphasis at this point is very much on *discussion* – these meetings should not be a case of 'put up or shut up'. If your headteacher, or anyone present at the meeting, requires clarification or further evidence of the judgements that have been made, this is the time to seek it.

According to *The Handbooks for Inspecting Schools*[1], feedback to senior managers in a school should include evidence and judgements about:

- the school's outcomes, particularly standards achieved by pupils;
- factors that account most for what is achieved, particularly strengths and weaknesses in teaching in the school;

- effectiveness of work done by managers and co-ordinators;
- issues identified by inspection as priorities for improving the school.

Feedback must also be given to the 'appropriate authority' (i.e. the governing body in most cases). Once again, the skills of the inspectors involved are crucial to how effectively their message is put across, and the extent to which the findings of the inspection are accepted by the governing body.

It is imperative that formal feedback meetings take place *before* the final inspection report is completed. One reason for this is to offer the opportunity for discussion on the findings and to allow for any necessary negotiation to take place. Only if a professional dialogue is not achieved (i.e. if disagreements arise early on and antagonisms develop) will feedback be curtailed.

Within six weeks of the end of the inspection, your registered inspector must have written a full inspection report and summary.

If your school had a short inspection, the report will be a commentary on what your school does well and where it could improve. Summaries of inspection reports must be no more than four pages long, '*readable and informative*'.

Inspectors are given clear guidance on how your inspection report should be written. According to the Ofsted document *Inspecting Schools: The Framework*[2]:

> *The text, balance and tone of the report must reflect the individual school as it is. The report must follow the prescribed structure, but its content and wording must not follow any pre-determined formula. Reports should be well argued, written in plain English and based convincingly on the evidence gathered before and during the inspection. They should provide the school with a clear basis for action. They should focus on what the school achieves and seek to explain why the standards achieved are as they are and what could be improved.*

Your headteacher will be sent a copy of the final report before it is published. This is so that s/he can check it for factual accuracy. If a factual inaccuracy exists, the final judgements will only be revised if the inaccuracy has a direct bearing on them. For most schools, the final inspection report will highlight many positive aspects of work and identify many strengths as well as some areas for improvement.

In short, the report and its summary should (according to *The Handbooks for Inspecting Schools*):

- be clear to all its readers, governors, parents, professionals and the public at large;
- concentrate on evaluating rather then describing what is seen;
- focus on the educational standards achieved and the factors which impact on standards and quality;
- use everyday language, not educational jargon, and be grammatically correct;
- be specific in its judgements;
- use sub-headings, bullet points and other devices to help to make the messages clear;
- use telling examples drawn from the evidence base to make generalisations understandable, and to illustrate what is meant by 'good' or 'poor';
- employ words and phrases that enliven the report and convey the individual character of the school.

Post-inspection stages for your school

When the inspection report arrives, it will contain a four-page summary which must be sent out by your governors to the parents/carers of all pupils. According to the Ofsted *Framework*, this summary will tell parents:

- what sort of school it is;
- what the school does well;
- what could be improved;
- how much the school has improved since the last inspection;
- how high standards are;
- how good the teaching is;
- how well the school looks after its pupils;

- how well the school works with parents;
- how well the school is led and managed;
- what parents think of the school and how far inspectors agree or disagree and why.

Your governors must also prepare an action plan that responds to the report within 40 working days of receiving it. This action plan must detail what your school plans to do in response to the section of the inspection report headed '*What should the school do to improve further?*'

The action plan must then be sent to parents of all pupils registered at your school (among others).

Inspection report in relation to teachers

For most classroom teachers, there is relatively little to do in the post-inspection stages until the action plan is complete and tasks for school improvement have been allocated. If you work in an area of your school that has been highlighted as being in need of particular development, you may well be consulted about how improvements can be achieved when the action plan is drawn up.

It is wise, if at all possible, to use this relative 'lull' to allow what has happened to sink in. No matter how skilfully the inspection has been managed by your school and the inspectors, experiencing an inspection should not be brushed aside as an insignificance – it *is* a challenging time for schools, and it *can* take its toll. Do not expect to bounce back to normal school life without even a little introspection after inspection.

School inspection survey

Once a school has been inspected, Ofsted will send a school inspection survey to be completed by your headteacher and one other randomly selected teacher. This is another way in which Ofsted can monitor the way in which schools view the process and quality of the inspection service offered to them.

From the analysis of these surveys, the latest statistics show that around 88–90 per cent of schools are satisfied with their inspection.

Approximately five per cent 'do not know', and around three to five per cent are not satisfied.

Your headteacher may well ask staff members for their views before s/he completes this form. Regardless of whether or not this is the case in your school, if you have a comment to make about any aspect of your experience of inspection, be sure to make it. Once again, feedback of this kind helps to contribute to the ongoing development of the inspection process.

Impact of the inspection

Regardless of the findings of the inspection team that visited your school, the experience will have an impact.

Impact on your school

The most obvious impact of inspection on your school is the requirement to draw up an action plan, and then to take those plans forward into tangible and assessable improvements. Without a genuine whole-school desire for self-improvement, this action plan cannot succeed. Even if there is a *developing* awareness of improvement needs, there will be an impact on your school.

Other impacts include the following:

1 If your school has achieved well in the inspection, there may be a pervading atmosphere of success and achievement. The contrary may be true if the inspection has highlighted more concerns than were expected.

2 Morale in your school may be boosted (although this can also take a bashing if the inspection was not as successful as anticipated).

3 Regardless of the outcome of an inspection, a common experience of schools seems to be a draining of energy like 'water down a plug'. Staff sickness rates have been known to soar, and although this cannot be helped it can greatly add to the pressures upon the remaining staff.

4 New habits of work may be set up by the inspection, either as a result of the self-scrutiny of the pre-inspection stages, or the report itself.

5 New directions of focus may be established or priorities for the future may be revised.

6 Unfortunately, in some schools, a culture of blame develops after an inspection; blame for what went wrong (if it did) and blame for areas of weakness. This is a clear sign that the senior management team is struggling. Blame does not equal support, encouragement and motivation. See the section on bullying on page 162 if you feel you are a victim of a culture of blame.

ABOUT

'BAD' INSPECTIONS

▶ It would be wrong to overlook the fact that, for some, inspection has a negative impact. While the schools in which this happens may not be placed on special measures or even designated as a school with serious weaknesses, if the overall outcome is a report that is not as positive as was expected, bad feeling can develop.

▶ This is always a sad outcome of an inspection, regardless of where the responsibility for the situation may lie. If the framework for inspection has been followed, there will have been good opportunities to address any differences of opinion as they arose, and seek to agree on a mutually pleasing result. Major shocks in the outcome of an inspection usually indicate either gross misconceptions on the part of the school regarding standards and achievements, or poor, if not incompetent, inspecting.

▶ The tasks facing schools with bad experiences are great. Morale must be rebuilt, and trust in those responsible for education policy and inspection re-established; not an easy job. Teamwork is essential in such schools if damage is to be limited, progress into the future made, and the pit of despair avoided.

▶ If this is your experience, you and your colleagues should be encouraged to take the support that may be forthcoming from within your school, as well as from without (perhaps from the local education authority, your union, any complaints procedures you choose to use, or helplines such as Teacherline).

7　There may be a movement of staff in the terms following an inspection, either to different positions within your school or to other posts outside your school.

8　Your school's standing in the local community may change as a result of the inspection.

9　Your school's relationship with the local education authority may alter – perhaps new pressures will develop or new avenues for discussion will be opened up.

Impact on your pupils

The pupils at your school will undoubtedly feel the impact of the inspection to a greater or lesser extent.

● If better practices are adopted as a result of the inspection, the quality of education offered should, and probably will, improve.

● The focus on effectiveness and social, moral, spiritual and cultural education that your school probably undertook will almost certainly have an impact on the lessons offered to pupils.

● Your school's policies (such as those on bullying and discrimination) may have been the subject of scrutiny, which in turn may lead to refinements that could improve the day-to-day experiences of pupils.

● Depending on the age of pupils at your school, they may now have a heightened awareness of the extent to which you strive to offer the best education possible.

Impact on you

Regardless of whether this is your first inspection or you have experienced several in the past (perhaps in different schools), there *will* be an impact on you personally. This may be a positively inspiring impact; it may also be the opposite. Here are some common experiences:

● There may be a need for immediate gratification straight after the inspection – many schools arrange some kind of party, or go out for a meal/drink etc. You may feel a need to treat yourself, and you should indulge!

THE IMPACT OF INSPECTIONS ON PUPILS

❭ Most pupils of secondary age, and possibly younger, seem to have a good idea of the impact that an inspection can have. In 1998, Market and Opinion Research International (MORI) carried out research on behalf of Ofsted into children's views on the impact of school inspections. Only 6 per cent felt that their school had got worse as a result of inspection, while 38 per cent felt that their school had improved. Fifty per cent felt that their school had remained the same after inspection.

❭ Interestingly, 39 per cent of pupils from schools that had been inspected said that they had spoken to an inspector in the process. About a third said that they spoke about their work, while 12 per cent spoke about the school in general (47 per cent did not speak to an inspector at all, and 11 per cent could not remember whether they had spoken to an inspector or not!). Of those who were aware of having been inspected, 62 per cent thought that they had learnt the same after the inspection as before, but 29 per cent thought that they had learnt more. 'Very few' felt that their learning had suffered as a result of inspection.

❭ This research concluded that Ofsted inspections '*appear on the whole to have made a positive contribution to standards in schools, according to the views of pupils*'. All very positive, but, perhaps most significantly for teachers facing an inspection, it is worth acknowledging the fact that pupils do make links between inspection and changes in the quality of education being offered to them.[3]

● You may feel physically tired – even exhausted. There is an inevitable amount of tension involved in inspection. Expelling this tension in a deflationary 'sigh of relief' can, ironically, result in a period of poor health.

● There may be a need to address areas for improvement at some stage in the future which will necessitate working more closely with leaders and managers. If you have a specific role to play in the action plan, you should be told exactly what that is. If it impacts on your workload significantly, your union may be able to offer some advice.

● There may be organisational changes in your school's structure and hierarchy as a result of the inspection, which will undoubtedly have an effect on working patterns and relationships.

One particularly common pitfall to avoid is the fact that when a development need is pointed out, it can be very easy to resist the change that is indicated; and so, directly or indirectly, the original criticism is rejected.

ABOUT

SETTING YOUR OWN TARGETS FOR IMPROVEMENT

▶ Although you will be a part of your school's action plan, you may feel that it is appropriate for you to set your own targets in response to the findings of the inspection and any self-evaluations undertaken.

▶ In advice given to schools on raising achievement through effective planning, West Sussex County Council makes the suggestion that targets should be SMART:

● **S**pecific (in relation to pupil achievement)

● **M**easurable (in terms of pupil progress and achievement)

● **A**chievable (within the resources of the school, including time and money)

● **R**elevant (to pupils and school aims)

● **T**ime-related (within a realistic time-span and with an identified end date)[4]

▶ This is a useful model to employ when looking at the issue of target setting. However, it is important to discuss what you are doing with your leaders and managers; they will want to ensure that you are not working contrary to the whole-school development plan, or that you are not being too hard on yourself!

Whether or not this is an issue for you, the quality of education being offered by you should not be negatively affected by inspection. If you believe that it has suffered, make your feelings known to your headteacher with (if possible) documentary evidence of how and why.

If you feel knocked off balance by the inspection, regardless of the outcome, take a moment to consider what it is that would help to restore your equilibrium. Perhaps you have a favourite book, place or person that you know can offer comfort; whatever it is, now would be a time to pursue what you know can make you feel better.

ABOUT

POST-INSPECTION SICKNESS

▸ The end of an inspection is no different from any other time of the school year regarding sickness. If you need to take time off, you must do so, with no thoughts of guilt or anxiety about the situation. No one is indispensable, and you will be of far more use to your school once you have recovered from whatever is causing you to feel unwell.

▸ If your illness lasts beyond the period of self-certification, you should mention to your doctor any factors that may have contributed to your health situation.

When a school is not achieving well enough

Some schools are deemed not to be achieving well enough. It is necessary for registered inspectors (with their teams) to judge:

- *Whether or not the school is failing, or is likely to fail, to give its pupils an acceptable standard of education, and thus require special measures;*

- *Whether or not the school, although providing an acceptable standard of education, nevertheless has serious weaknesses in one or more areas of its work;*

- *Whether or not the school, although not identified as having serious weaknesses, is judged to be underachieving.* [5]

If any of these scenarios apply to your school, there are specific procedures that inspectors must follow.

When a school requires 'special measures'

It is fair to say that there has been some savage delight from some quarters of the media in schools requiring special measures. However, it should be remembered that only around 3 per cent of schools have been found to be failing, or likely to fail, to provide an acceptable standard of education to their pupils, and therefore in need of special measures.

Section 13 (9) of The School Inspections Act 1996 states that: '*Special measures are required to be taken in relation to a school if the school is failing or likely to fail to give its pupils an acceptable standard of education*'. Your inspection team will be making this decision, but it must also be agreed by Her Majesty's Chief Inspector (HMCI) if special measures are required.

This decision is not taken lightly and is based on pre-inspection analysis of data, other indicators of your school's performance, as well as your inspection team's views following a full inspection. It is not an easy decision for an inspection team to make, and they are given clear guidance on how it should be reached. If your school has only one major weakness, it is highly unlikely that special measures will be invoked.

Inspectors are given the following chart (Table 7.1) to help them judge whether or not a school requires special measures (questions should be answered 'yes' or 'no'):

If it is decided that your school may require special measures, your registered inspector must first report his or her findings to the Ofsted School Improvement Division before your school is told. Your headteacher will then be informed during oral feedback at the end of the inspection, and it is usual for formal, prescribed language to be used. Then, a short time later, your governing body must be offered oral feedback on your inspection team's findings. A local education authority representative may be present at this meeting.

Table 7.1: Inspectors' guidelines on special measures for schools.

Education standards achieved	Quality of education provided	Leadership and management of the school
a Is there low achievement in the subjects of the Curriculum by the majority of pupils, or consistently among particular groups of pupils?	**a** Is there a high proportion of unsatisfactory teaching?	**a** Is the headteacher and/or the senior management team, and/or the governors, ineffective?
b Is there poor learning and progress in the subjects of the Curriculum by the majority of pupils or consistently among particular groups of pupils?	**b** Are there low expectations of pupils?	**b** Is there significant loss of confidence in the headteacher by the staff, and/or the parents, and/or the governors?
c Are there poor examination results?	**c** Is there failure to implement the National Curriculum?	**c** Is there demoralisation and disenchantment amongst staff?
d Are the National Curriculum assessment and other accredited results poor?	**d** Is there poor provision for pupils' spiritual, moral, social and cultural development?	**e** Are there high levels of staff turnover or absence?
e Is there regular disruptive behaviour?	**e** Are pupils at physical or emotional risk from other pupils or adults in the school?	**f** Is there poor management?
f Is there a breakdown of discipline?	**f** Are there abrasive or confrontational relationships between staff and pupils?	**g** Is inefficient use made of the resources available to the school, including finance?
		h Does the school apply principles of Best Value in its use of resources?

Table 7.1 *continued*

Education standards achieved	Quality of education provided	Leadership and management of the school
g Are there high levels of exclusions?		
h Are there significant levels of racial tension or harassment?		
i Is there poor attendance by a substantial proportion of pupils?		
j Is there poor attendance by particular groups of pupils?		
k Is there a high level of truancy?		

Adapted from the *Handbook for Inspecting Primary and Nursery Schools*, p. 167.

As a draft inspection report must be sent to HMCI, the publication of the final report may be delayed by up to three months. It is then up to HMCI to decide whether or not to place your school on special measures. He may decide to send a team of HMI to your school to gather more information. If such a visit is deemed necessary, it will take place within three working weeks of the Ofsted inspection. If HMCI disagrees with your registered inspector having examined the evidence available, his or her decision takes precedence.

If the final decision is that your school does require special measures, both the DfEE and Ofsted will contact your governing body and local education authority with guidance on the next steps. As a teacher at a school requiring special measures, it is really important to wait for the dissemination of information within your school, rather than comparing your situation with other schools in a similar position. This is because no two schools are exactly the same, and such comparisons will undoubtedly lead to confusion and anxiety.

Although this is easier said than done, do not fall into despair about the situation. No one would deny that a school facing special measures has challenges ahead and the path will certainly not be easy, but it will be a period of great change and hopefully positive development. You would be right to expect improvements in your working conditions, and also to expect that the staff in your school will necessarily be brought closer together in a common purpose.

Depending on the circumstances of your school, either your governing body or your local education authority will draw up an action plan (which is the key management tool for improvement) to address the key issues identified by the inspectors. This plan must be submitted to the Secretary of State and HMCI within 40 working days of receiving the final inspection report.

According to Circular No. 06/99, *Schools Causing Concern*, the action plan submitted by your school should '*have a timetable which will allow the school to be removed from special measures as soon as possible and no later than two years from the date of receipt of the inspection report*'[6]. For each issue identified by the inspection report, the action plan should state:

– what is to be done (in terms of clear and specific actions);
– who is to do it (who is responsible for ensuring the action takes place, and who else is involved);
– when it will be done (time scale with key milestones);
– what resources are required (in particular, how the school intends to use the Standards Fund Grant, including funding for teacher development);

- success criteria (quantitative targets, where possible) against which progress will be judged;
- how progress will be monitored (by whom, when and how) and;
- how progress will be evaluated (by whom, when and how).

Your school will also be issued with the Special Measures Guidance Pack.

HMI will visit your school to monitor progress during the period that it is in special measures. The first visit usually occurs six months after a school is inspected, and the purpose is for HMI to make judgements on:

● *The quality of the action plan and the local education authority statement;*

● *The local education authority's target date for when the school will be ready to be removed from special measures;*

● *The effectiveness of the current and future local education authority support to the school;*

● *Progress since the initial inspection which put the school under special measures[7].*

The judgements that HMI make will be reported to your headteacher, the Secretary of State, your governing body and your local education authority. It may then be necessary for your school to issue a revised action plan. Usually HMI visit schools in special measures once a term. When notice is given of such a visit, your headteacher and governors will need to prepare a summary of improvements made to your school, and a self-evaluation of progress made against each issue identified by Ofsted.

Being removed from special measures

There are two ways out of special measures: to close, or to be judged by HMI to be offering pupils an acceptable standard of education.

If, following a visit from HMI, it is decided that your school no longer requires special measures, a further short inspection of a couple of days will be made. If it is still decided that your school can be removed from special measures, it will be issued with a new inspection report to that end.

There are general indicators of recovery for schools in special measures that have been laid out in the Ofsted leaflet *Removal from Special Measures* (available free of charge on tel. no. 020 7510 0180). These indicators include:

1 A year-on-year increase in the proportion of pupils entered for and passing GCSEs.

2 Sustained improvement in the numbers of pupils achieving age-appropriate levels in National Curriculum tests.

3 At least satisfactory progress of pupils in three-quarters or more of their lessons.

4 Improvements in attitudes, behaviour and personal development.

5 A reduction in the number of exclusions.

6 Improvements in attendance.

7 Satisfactory or better teaching in three-quarters or more of lessons.

8 Significant improvements in leadership and management.

Your school may also be removed from special measures if it has closed and reopened as a 'Fresh Start' school.

Removal from special measures does not necessarily mean that weaknesses no longer exist, but it does mean that a school has been deemed to be well placed to continue making improvements. It is an occasion for celebration at the significant achievements of your school and its staff.

The Ofsted booklet *From Failure to Success* (available free of charge on tel. no. 020 7510 0180) makes interesting reading for anyone concerned with special measures, as does *Lessons Learned from Special Measures*, available on the same number.

ABOUT

DEALING WITH FAILURE

'What we call failure is not the falling down but the staying down.'
Mary Pickford

▶ If you are working in a school that has been deemed to be failing to provide an adequate standard of education, there is a need to focus on ways of bringing success into the school's psyche, rather than failure. It can be difficult not to let the situation have a direct effect on your personal self-worth and self-esteem.

▶ Ofsted has noticed that, following placement on special measures, schools often experience emotions 'akin to grieving'. Anger and resentment are common stages in the grieving process, but when directed at the status of special measures these emotions may do little to help move the school forward, and a lot in attempting to apportion blame.

▶ It is not helpful to consider *yourself* as a failure. It is the school in which you work that has been deemed to have failed, and the work you do in that school is dependent upon so many different factors, not least the dynamics between every member of staff. The quicker your school can actively launch into its programme of improvements, the quicker you will emerge successfully from special measures. At their most positive, these improvements will offer the potential for exciting regeneration that could be a thoroughly fulfilling experience.

▶ If you are finding it difficult to move away from the notion of failure, try speaking to the most positive members of staff to find out how and why they are viewing the situation in the way they are. Your headteacher may also be able to offer some encouragement, as may your local education authority's confidential stress line (if it has one). You could also try focusing on an area of change that needs to be made and that can be achieved relatively easily. Congratulate yourself and others on *every* success! Do remember that this is a temporary situation. Whatever the end-result, your school will not be on special measures indefinitely.

Working in a school under special measures

There is no doubt that working in a school under special measures will be a challenge, but many teachers who have experienced this feel positive that the often impossible circumstances in which they have had to function in the past are going to be fully addressed. That said, feelings of de-professionalisation seem to be an issue for some teachers in this situation.

If this is a possibility for you, just remember that working in a school with known and identified difficulties could be said to draw on a higher level of professionalism than any other sort of school! These ideas may help:

- Contact your union as soon as you hear that your school has been placed on special measures, as it may have guidance for members working in such schools.

- Some schools that have been placed on special measures experience a high turnover of staff, as teachers decide to leave the school rather than stay through the inevitable changes. Think carefully about your position on this. If you decide to remain at your school while others choose to leave, consider the impact this may have on your work as new colleagues join you and staffing restabilises. If you decide to leave, do so with positivity; do not feel that you are leaving a 'sinking ship'. You are, of course, entitled to make whatever decision suits you, but do inform your headteacher as soon as you make it.

- Consider how you and your colleagues view your school. Is this an opportunity to thrive or a time of *failure*? If the 'failing' label has taken hold, be aware that this can take time to dissipate.

Be prepared for continued observations. If this presents any problems for you, speak to your headteacher. It may be possible to arrange some additional observations by a 'critical friend' who is in a position to support you through this phase. Some schools in special measures arrange for staff to take part in mentoring partnerships.

Be prepared for a fairly rapid pace of change. This can be unsettling, but if you recognise such feelings as they arise, and discuss them with colleagues and leaders/managers, change should not lead to excessive anxiety or discomfort. Expect new policies on key aspects, such as behaviour management and attendance, and possibly an individual action plan setting out clear targets for each member of staff.

If stress becomes problematic during this period, do not suffer in silence. Speak to your union, Teacherline and your chosen healthcare provider for practical advice and perspective. If it is any consolation, some teachers report a certain level of exhilaration at the opportunity for their school – in which they have invested time, effort and energy – to make a fresh start.

Research by the National Federation for Educational Research in 1999[8] found that teachers and headteachers in special measures schools were more likely to work longer hours than their equivalents in other schools. For headteachers, the average number of hours worked each week was 63 against 58 at other schools, and for teachers these figures were 56 hours against 53. Of course, all these figures are too high, but be particularly aware of the impact on your work/life balance of rising working hours, and do everything in your power to preserve your precious non-work time.

In the report *Lessons Learned from Special Measures*, Ofsted has recognised that '*The teachers who suffer most in the early days of the school being in special measures are often those who always do a thorough job and whose teaching is consistently good. During the period of special measures, this group of teachers usually develops even better teaching skills and make a major contribution to driving the school forward by serving as exemplars of good practice*'. Food for thought!

It is usually the case that primary schools can be removed from special measures quicker than secondary schools. This is perhaps because of the size of secondary schools, and the fact that progress is necessarily slower.

Features for success in a school under special measures

The Ofsted report *Lessons Learned from Special Measures* sets out the main features of what works in improving schools quickly. These features are reproduced below (Table 7.2):

Table 7.2: Outline of improving schools quickly. Adapted from Ofsted's report *Lessons Learned from Special Measures*.

Getting started	Coming to terms with the inspection findings quickly.
	Involving all staff and governors, and at times parents and pupils, in the compilation and implementation of the action plan.
	Keeping the needs of the pupils at the top of the list of priorities as progress is reviewed.
A better deal for pupils	Celebrating pupils' achievements.
	Raising pupils' self-esteem, and improving their skills as learners.
	Establishing ways to check that standards are improving, and knowing the levels to which they ought to rise.
Promoting positive attitudes	Tackling pupils' inappropriate behaviour, and encouraging self-control.
	Finding ways to help pupils to come to school every day, and to do so punctually.
	Setting up a system for monitoring attendance and punctuality, under the leadership of a senior member of staff.
The way ahead for teachers and support staff	Concentrating on setting learning objectives for each lesson.
	Establishing a common approach to planning, to simplify the workload and employ an efficient and effective system.

Table 7.2 *continued*

	Using the strengths of individual members of staff productively.
	Agreeing and following a common policy for assessment.
Role of co-ordinators and support staff	Ensuring the subject matter to be taught is clearly defined in the Curriculum overview, schemes of work, long-term and termly plans.
	Evaluating the effectiveness of the department's contribution to whole school issues.
	Contributing to a team approach to tackling the school's problems.
Headteachers and senior managers moving forward	Providing clear-sighted and dynamic leadership.
	Monitoring, recognising, improving and rewarding achievement.
	Providing guidance about lesson planning, teaching methods, standards and good-quality teaching.
	Analysing the results of tests and examinations to reveal where specific weaknesses lie.
	Monitoring the teaching, and evaluating this information to guide decisions about spending, staffing, grouping pupils and training.
	Evaluating the findings of external monitors, and adjusting the schools' priorities in response to them.
Governors taking the lead	Securing the services of an effective headteacher, or acting headteacher.
	Having some involvement in the routine work of the school.
	Questioning senior staff about decisions they have taken or should take.

Table 7.2 *continued*

	Using governors' meetings effectively, to monitor progress in implementing the action plan and to increase knowledge of school management.
	Managing the procedures for determining the competence of staff.
Moving forward with parents	Welcoming parents and volunteer helpers to support pupils, and providing them with training to fulfil that role.
	Encouraging parents and carers to enter into an educational partnership with the school.
	Helping parents to understand what pupils are taught in school.
	Giving parents a role to play within the school's homework policy.
Making full use of external support	Ensuring that local education authority officers provide a good balance of advice, training and monitoring.
	Securing the provision of expert staff seconded to the school to take leading roles in addressing weaknesses.
	Using materials and ideas that have been developed in other schools, local education authorities, universities or publications.
Coming out of special measures and moving on	Maintaining a forward momentum to school
	Establishing a plan for phased withdrawal of extra support, to ensure self-sufficiency as soon as possible
	Ensuring a smooth transition, for both staff and pupils, from a school that is closing to a new placement.

'To be truly radical is to make hope possible rather than despair convincing.' RAYMOND WILLIAMS

If your school has serious weaknesses

Some schools may not fall into the 'special measures' category, but are deemed to have serious weaknesses nevertheless. Ofsted estimates that about ten per cent of schools fall into this category. The Circular 6/99 says that a school has serious weaknesses if the registered inspector states in the inspection report that the school, '*although giving its pupils, in general, an acceptable standard of education, has significant weaknesses in one or more areas of its activities*'. This is a judgement that your inspection team is entitled to make without seeking corroboration from HMCI, and is likely to if your school has the following weaknesses:

- *Low standards of achievement and/or unsatisfactory learning and progress made, particularly in the core subjects;*
- *Unsatisfactory teaching in about one in eight lessons;*
- *Ineffective leadership and/or management* [9]

Should this be the verdict for your school, your headteacher will be given an oral feedback. A representative from your local education authority may be present at this meeting. Then, within six weeks of the inspection, your registered inspector will send a written report to your school and governing body, your local education authority and HMCI.

At this stage, Ofsted will provide guidance on how your school should proceed in order to take the action necessary to address the weaknesses. As a staff member, you should expect to be closely involved in the drawing up of an action plan that focuses on the key issues identified by Ofsted. This action plan must be submitted by your governing body to HMCI within 40 working days of receiving the final inspection report. This action plan should take the same format as an action plan for a school in special measures. Your local education authority will also submit a statement of action to HMCI.

In order to help your school improve, your local education authority will have access to the School Improvement Grant. When it is satisfied that your school's action plan is sound, it will pass this grant on to your school. The DfEE would only be involved if HMI are not satisfied that the grant can lead to the necessary improvements after they have looked at your school's action plan.

At least once a term afterwards, your local education authority will discuss progress with your school and record its assessment of progress to date. If, after six months, your school is still not making sufficient progress, your local education authority will have to use its powers of intervention. These powers are described in the Circular 6/99.

Once your school has been designated as having serious weaknesses, it has about two years to make the necessary improvements. If it does not achieve this in time for another visit from a registered inspector, it is likely to be placed on special measures.

When a school is a cause for concern

Your local education authority does not need to wait for a visit from Ofsted inspectors to identify schools that have become a cause for concern. It can, using the same criteria as Ofsted, issue a school with a formal warning about the weaknesses that it has. If the school does not respond to this warning in sufficient ways, your local education authority does have the power to place the school either in the category requiring special measures, or in the category of schools with serious weaknesses.

Your local education authority is likely to issue your school with a formal warning if:

- *The standards of performance of pupils at the school are unacceptably low and are likely to remain so unless the local education authority appoints additional governors and/or suspends the school's delegated budget;*
- *There has been a serious breakdown in the way that the school is managed or governed which is prejudicing, or is likely to prejudice, pupils' standards of performance; or*
- *The safety of pupils or staff of the school is threatened, whether by breakdown of discipline or otherwise* [10].

A formal warning will only be issued to your school if your school has been previously informed about your local education authority's concerns and has not taken sufficient action to remedy the situation.

Utilising the feedback received

Having been through the experience of an inspection and heard the immediate feedback that inspectors have given you, it is really important to pull out of the information you have received the threads that can lead to future improvement. This is perhaps one of the most difficult aspects of the post-inspection phase as, understandably, the natural inclination is to get back to normal for a while. Facing new developments, and even learning new competencies, usually takes a level of enthusiasm that can be hard to locate amongst the recently inspected!

For this reason, it is essential to give yourself a 'break'. Your inspection may have finished on a Friday, and the following Monday you are immediately back working at full pelt again (probably having even worked over the weekend), but to throw in new goals for development from day one will undoubtedly prove self-destructive. Unless you move to a different school (or your present school is placed on special measures), your next inspection will be some years away and you will have plenty of time to digest the effects of what you have been through. In fact, some schools advocate waiting as long as half a term before focusing on development needs once the post-inspection stages have been completed. At least this way you will have time to assimilate the information that your inspection provided you with.

Here are some ideas on utilising the feedback received from an inspection.

1 Make sure that any feedback given does not contradict advice from other agencies. Openly discuss any contradictory advice you have been given.

2 Aim to be absolutely clear about the implications of each point made in the inspection report. If you need clarification on anything, seek it from

ABOUT

YOUR SCHOOL'S ACTION PLAN

❯ The most tangible way of utilising the feedback received from an inspection will be the creation of an action plan for future development. The purpose of this plan is to ensure that all the points flagged up for development in the inspection report are addressed, with clear responsibilities for action, success, monitoring and evaluation identified. In brief, this action plan must:

- respond point-by-point to the findings of the inspection report;
- set out measurable indicators of improvement;
- be able to make an impact on *quality* and *standards*;
- be devised with those who must implement it in mind;
- involve governors, parents, pupils and all staff;
- estimate what demands will be made of staff and other resources of the school;
- set out clear time-scales in which action should be taken;
- contribute to ongoing self-evaluation;
- be achievable.

❯ Do not let the action plan be done *to* you. If you have any major part to play in the improvements targeted by the plan, make sure that you have the opportunity to discuss the finer details of how success might be achieved and what support might be forthcoming.

❯ Your overall workload should not increase significantly.

❯ Do be aware that lasting success in any area of your school's work cannot be fully achieved in isolation, without the backing of the entire school community. The most important tools here will be good teaching and effective management.

your leaders or headteacher. Do not leave any room for potential confusion. You should not be personally identifiable in the report, but if you feel that you are (perhaps you are the only person with certain responsibilities), and you have concerns about what has been written, talk to your union and leaders/managers about it.

3 Consider carefully whether there is a need for professional development training. Put your case forward as early as possible, as resources may be limited!

4 Think about whether or not there should be some changes made to the set-up in which you work. Are you working under unrealistic (or incomparable) pressures? Does your situation need reviewing?

5 Make sure that there is not a mismatch between any areas highlighted for development that involve you, and your involvement in the action plan. Targets must be agreed so that future problems are avoided.

6 Seek to keep discussions going within your school, so that a shared vision for improvement (where all carry responsibility for success) prevails. This helps to avoid the development of a culture of blame.

7 Be prepared to push out the boundaries of success in the areas that have been highlighted as being in need of development. Pose challenging questions about your role in the improvements that are to be made.

8 Take time to appreciate all the successes that you and your school have achieved.

9 Recognise that it is teachers, backed up by strong leadership and management, who are the agents of change. Inspection in itself cannot improve a school.

10 Do not expect to make improvements overnight. This takes time, and the notion of development and possible change needs to sink down into the psyche of each and every one within your school community; teachers and learners alike. At the same time, do not let improvement processes drift. If you are asked how long you think an improvement might take to implement, always overestimate! Underestimation is often the source of unprecedented stress. Remember, too, that development can take place in the short-, medium- and long-term.

11 Make sure you understand the reasoning behind any changes that are implemented. This will help to avoid questioning the legitimacy of directives from above. If you disagree with decisions made, take the time to discuss your views with trusted colleagues to see if others will support you when you make your views known to your leaders and managers. Do not simply accept what happens if you have genuine objections, as this may stunt real growth for your school.

12 There can be no such thing as 'mastery'. As soon as an individual or institution reaches a particular level, yet higher plains of competency come into view. However, it is the knowledge that there is no such thing as 'perfection' that puts schools and teachers in the best position for appropriate development. Being open to learning and change is a true sign of success. If the feedback you receive encourages reflection, your purpose will almost certainly be refined.

13 Remember that it can be the subtlest of changes that can bring about the most dramatic improvements.

ABOUT

WHEN DEVELOPMENT NEEDS ARE NOT PICKED UP DURING AN INSPECTION

➤ Although this should be a rare occurrence, it has been known for inspections to miss what the staff of a school consider to be areas that need development. Whatever the reasons for this, there is clearly a dilemma here. What to do? Reveal the 'guilty secret', or keep quiet in the awareness of the fact that the final report is a public document?

➤ This book cannot offer a solution, but it was pointed out by one school with this experience that, once the 'phew' factor had faded, the knowledge that the original problem still existed was stronger than ever before!

Evaluating your inspection experience

'Things turn out best for the people who make the best of the way things turn out.' ART LINKLETTER

Your school will probably want to carry out some form of evaluation on how well you all coped with the inspection (after all, there cannot be a reflective practitioner in the land who does not strive for increasingly better ways of doing things). The main aims of such processes of evaluation are to define what went well and what should perhaps be done differently next time.

For your part in this process, these ideas may help:

1 Keep a note of any aspect of the inspection that has caused you anxiety. Be as specific as possible, and record what helped you and what hindered you. Aim to re-read what you write the next time you receive notice of an inspection, as it may help you to avoid a recurrence. Think of this exercise as advice to your future self!

2 Consider what knowledge of yourself you have gained through the inspection. Has it taught you anything about the way in which you handle such situations, or has it extended your self-understanding?

3 Take a moment or two to reflect on the school in which you work, now that it is in its post-inspection phase. Are you in an environment where you can flourish? Are you and the school 'compatible'?

4 What about your contribution to the school? Are you a key member of staff who could offer more? Can you see your relative position more clearly? Has an unofficial hierarchy developed or been exploded as a result of the inspection?

5 Were there any aspects of observation and scrutiny that concerned you? What would make you feel more comfortable about this process?

Do remember that, as a teacher (and as an individual), you amount to so much more than the judgement given to you on your teaching performance. In fact, this was never meant to *define* or identify you, but merely to state where you are at present, not where you will be even in a term's time. Do not be contained or limited by the feedback you are given. However positive (or negative) it was, you can go beyond it and flourish further. Take the long view, welcome any changes that are necessary, and celebrate what you do well.

Getting back to normal

Well, what is normal? Many schools report that life is not the same after an inspection, and this is not necessarily a bad thing. As long as the experience has not left you gasping for breath, utterly deflated and bereft, the changes brought about may be refreshingly welcome.

- Aim to include an ongoing evaluation of your work as part of your definition of 'normal'. Do not go too long without requesting some form of observation by peers, leaders or managers.

- Focus on *identified* priorities, rather than anything else. You do not need to storm ahead, all guns blazing; allow time for the dust to settle and the future direction to become clear.

- Make a note of any procedural/organisational changes that you would like to make as a result of the inspection, however small they may be.

- Be sure to reinstate any events/treats/trips that were postponed until after the inspection.

- Avoid prolonged debate with pupils about the inspection. Many headteachers like to address some of the issues raised by the inspection with pupils, and it is usually best not to add to this in your own classroom, if possible.

Coping with post-inspection stress

Ironically, once the inspection is over, many teachers seem to experience feelings of stress. Although you might feel that the stress should have been relieved as the inspectors leave the school premises, there are some aspects of this stage of the process that can prove difficult for susceptible people.

- *Change:* There will almost certainly be some aspect of change at your school following inspection, even if the outcome was overwhelmingly positive. While this change may bring progress and improvement, it can be unsettling and demanding, as adjustments must be made.

- *New job roles:* The weeks following your inspection may see alterations to your job. Even if you welcome this, there may be an element of stress involved as you adjust to the new expectations.

- *Insufficient feedback about the next steps:* There will be action to take in response to the inspection report, but this can be made difficult by inefficient communication between managers/leaders and staff.

Reactions to the end of an inspection vary about as much as the people involved! These stress busting ideas may help you:

1 Make a mental break once the inspection is over. Do not take the feelings associated with this time forward into the future.

2 Even if the outcome of the inspection was beyond your wildest dreams (in a positive sense), do not be surprised if you feel the effects of stress. Good things can be stressful, too. Just think about committing to a new partner, having a baby, moving house, and so on.

3 Watch out for unexpected behaviour. Some teachers who have suffered inspection stress find themselves behaving in unusual ways – do not give yourself a hard time, but do seek advice from your healthcare provider if you are concerned.

EXAMPLE: I was so pleased about the way the inspection had gone. I had got on well with the inspectors, and the feedback was all very positive. But when I went home on the final day I cried and cried. I felt terrible all weekend, and felt really annoyed with myself for not feeling a sense of relief. I had not realised how much tension I had stored up, and I suppose this was just my way of releasing it. I do not want to get into that state again. I had not realised what had happened until it was too late.

---

4 Your inner resilience has taken a knock if you are feeling the effects of negative stress after an inspection, and you need to pay back your 'overdraft'! Draw too heavily on your inner resources without replenishing them and the charges will be high. Be kind to yourself now; get as much rest as possible, and adjust your expectations of yourself to take account of your feelings.

5 Try not to feel contained and dominated by the whole experience. Stay connected with your purpose at work while you focus on the future.

ACTION: Aim to learn as much as you can from your experience of inspection. Write down what caused you stress and how you attempted to alleviate it. What worked and what did not? How would you do things differently in the future?

6 Resume your work/life balance (if it was knocked off centre) as soon as possible after the inspection. If you felt, or still feel, extreme stress, this is unacceptable. You should seek the advice of your healthcare provider with the intention of nurturing your mental and physical health. Try to convey to leaders/managers, and possibly to Ofsted itself (if a complaint is deemed necessary) the extent of your suffering.

7 Remember that the human body is capable of learning that what once stressed it did not kill it. If the stressor (i.e. the inspection) is repeated, the negative effects can be more subdued.

ABOUT

BULLYING AFTER AN INSPECTION

● In a very small minority of cases, teachers have found that, once the inspectors leave their school, the bullying begins. Leaders and managers feel under pressure to bring about swift improvements to the quality of education being offered, and someone has to be a scapegoat. Thankfully, this attitude is rare, but it can happen.

● If you feel that you are being bullied as a result of the inspection, read the information on page 162 about adult bullying. Do remember, too, that an Ofsted inspection is not sufficient evidence of incompetence, and that the judgements made on your teaching should not be used in any way other than supportive.

● Do not tolerate bullying. It is illegal and always without justification.

Making complaints *after* an inspection

Once the inspection has been completed and the post-inspection stages have passed, the only complaints left are likely to be in response to the final written report. This is very rare, as complaints at this late stage reflect the fact that the built-in mechanisms for raising complaints before this stage were either not utilised or not effective.

If you still have an outstanding complaint to make after the inspection has been completed, discuss the matter with your headteacher.

Remember to document the nature of, and reasons for, your complaint, what you have done to resolve the situation, and the solution you would wish for.

Complaints made after the inspection may also be in response to the fact that complaints made earlier on in the process have not been resolved by the registered inspector or contractor. *Do not let the matter drop if you have a genuine concern.*

If your headteacher has raised an issue with the registered inspector and a resolution has not been achieved, the contractor must step in. If this still results in dissatisfaction, it would be appropriate to take the step of lodging a formal complaint with Ofsted, adding the point of incompetence with which the situation has been handled to the original complaint. You should *always* hear the result, conclusion or outcome of *any* complaints made at *any* level. This is simple courtesy.

Overall, only two to three per cent of inspections result in a formal complaint to Ofsted being made. Whether this is reflective of a high level of satisfaction with the inspection system as a whole, or the skill with which registered inspectors handle complaints put to them during the actual inspection, is very difficult to know. What is clear is that this is the feedback received from those who have experienced school inspections. This contributes to the ongoing refinements made to the framework for inspection. If there is any comment that you wish to make about any stage of the inspection process, do make your views known.

---

1   TSO, 1999.

2   Ofsted, 1999.

3   These statistics were taken from *The Impact of School Inspections – Children's Views (A Research Study Among 11–16 Year Olds)*, January–February 1998.

4   WSCC, *Raising Achievement Through Effective Planning*, 1996.

5   *Inspecting Schools, The Framework*, Ofsted 1999.

---

6   This circular is available to download from the DfEE website, **www.dfee.gov.uk** or from the DfEE Publications Centre on tel. no. 0845 602 22 60.

7   Circular number 06/99, *Schools Causing Concern.*

8   *The Impact of Ofsted Inspections* by Margaret Scanlon.

9   *The Handbooks for Inspecting Schools*, TSO, 1999.

10   Circular 6/99.

Primary parents' questionnaire

Parents' Questionnaire

```
┌────────────────────────────────┐
│                                │
│                                │
└────────────────────────────────┘
```

Name of school being inspected

This questionnaire is being sent to all parents with children at the school. Please fill it in so that the inspection team can have your views of the school. Your answers and comments are confidential to the inspection team. They will not be seen by the school, but a summary of the views of parents as a whole will be included in the inspection report.

If you have more than one child at the school, please fill in a separate questionnaire for each as your views on some things may differ from child to child.

Please give the age of the child to which these views refer:

☐ Years

For each of the statements below, please tick the box which best reflects your views of the school.

		Strongly agree	Tend to agree	Tend to disagree	Strongly disagree	Don't know
1	My child likes school	☐	☐	☐	☐	☐
2	My child is making good progress in school	☐	☐	☐	☐	☐
3	Behaviour in the school is good	☐	☐	☐	☐	☐
4	My child gets the right amount of work to do at home	☐	☐	☐	☐	☐
5	The teaching is good	☐	☐	☐	☐	☐

Parents' Questionnaire (primary) *continued*

	Strongly agree	Tend to agree	Tend to disagree	Strongly disagree	Don't know
6 I am kept well informed about how my child is getting on	☐	☐	☐	☐	☐
7 I would feel comfortable about approaching the school with questions or a problem	☐	☐	☐	☐	☐
8 The school expects my child to work hard to achieve his or her best	☐	☐	☐	☐	☐
9 The school works closely with parents	☐	☐	☐	☐	☐
10 The school is well led and managed	☐	☐	☐	☐	☐
11 The school is helping my child become mature and responsible	☐	☐	☐	☐	☐
12 The school provides an interesting range of activities outside lessons	☐	☐	☐	☐	☐

If you wish to comment further on these or any other matters about the school, either its strengths or its weaknesses, you can use the back of this questionnaire or write a separate letter.

Thank you for taking the time to fill in this questionnaire. Please return it in a sealed envelope to the registered inspector. The school will tell you how to do this.

_____   _____

Signature of parent (optional)   Date

Secondary parents' questionnaire

Parents' Questionnaire

Name of school being inspected

This questionnaire is being sent to all parents with children at the school. Please fill it in so that the inspection team can have your views of the school. Your answers and comments are confidential to the inspection team. They will not be seen by the school, but a summary of the views of parents as a whole will be included in the inspection report.

If you have more than one child at the school, please fill in a separate questionnaire for each as your views on some things may differ from child to child.

Please give the age of the child to which these views refer:

☐ Years

For each of the statements below, please tick the box which best reflects your views of the school.

		Strongly agree	Tend to agree	Tend to disagree	Strongly disagree	Don't know
1	My child likes school	☐	☐	☐	☐	☐
2	My child is making good progress in school	☐	☐	☐	☐	☐
3	Behaviour in the school is good	☐	☐	☐	☐	☐
4	My child gets the right amount of work to do at home	☐	☐	☐	☐	☐
5	The teaching is good	☐	☐	☐	☐	☐

Parents' Questionnaire (secondary) *continued*

	Strongly agree	Tend to agree	Tend to disagree	Strongly disagree	Don't know
6 I am kept well informed about how my child is getting on	☐	☐	☐	☐	☐
7 I would feel comfortable about approaching the school with questions or a problem	☐	☐	☐	☐	☐
8 The school expects my child to work hard to achieve his or her best	☐	☐	☐	☐	☐
9 The school works closely with parents	☐	☐	☐	☐	☐
10 The school is well led and managed	☐	☐	☐	☐	☐
11 The school is helping my child become mature and responsible	☐	☐	☐	☐	☐
12 The school provides an interesting range of activities outside lessons	☐	☐	☐	☐	☐

If you wish to comment further on these or any other matters about the school, either its strengths or its weaknesses, you can use the back of this questionnaire or write a separate letter.

Thank you for taking the time to fill in this questionnaire. Please return it in a sealed envelope to the registered inspector. The school will tell you how to do this.

_____   _____

Signature of parent (optional)   Date

_____

Authority letter to secondary parents

Draft letter for the appropriate authority to send to parents to notify them of the meeting for parents.

Name and address of the appropriate authority

Dear Parent or Guardian

Inspection of (school)

Notice of meeting for parents (time, date, place)

As you may already know, this school is soon to be inspected as part of the programme of regular school inspections arranged by Her Majesty's Chief Inspector of Schools. The inspection will be carried out by a team led by (name), a registered inspector.

This letter is to invite you to attend a meeting with the registered inspector which is being held before the inspection. The meeting is open to all parents of pupils at the school and the governors and staff will not be present during the meeting unless they also have children at the school. The purpose of the meeting is for you to tell the registered inspector your views about the school and how it works so that these views can be included in the inspection. Although the registered inspector will want to hear your views, and will attempt to answer your questions, he or she will not be in a position to comment on your views, which will be taken account of in the inspection. The registered inspector will also be able to tell you about the inspection. The agenda for the meeting is attached to this letter; you may find it helpful to read it now and if possible bring it to the meeting.

The registered inspector has also asked us to send a questionnaire to all parents for them to complete and return to him/her. The questionnaire is being sent out with this letter. The questionnaire is additional to the parents' meeting, and covers much the same ground. Please do fill in whether or not you can attend the meeting. The questionnaire is confidential between you and the registered inspector. The school does not see individual answers, but the overall findings will be included in the inspection report. If you want to write in more detail to the registered inspector, please do so, preferably before the meeting. The questionnaire and any letters should be sent to:

(Name and address of the registered inspector or name of the registered inspector, c/o of the school)

I hope you will be able to come to the meeting.

Yours faithfully

For the Appropriate Authority

Secondary parents' meeting agenda

Parents meeting

Name of school:

Date of meeting: Time:

Agenda

1   Introduction by registered inspector.

2   Discussion on the following topics:

- the standards the school achieves;

- how the school helps pupils, whatever their ability, to learn and make progress;

- the attitudes and values the school promotes;

- behaviour and attendance;

- the work the school expects pupils to do at home, the school's links with parents – including information on how pupils are getting on;

- how the school responds to parents' suggestions and concerns;

- how the school has improved in recent years.

3   Any other issues that parents may wish to raise.

Further reading

It is a good idea to keep up-to-date with the latest publications from Ofsted, regardless of whether or not you have an inspection pending. A full list of available publications can be found on the Ofsted website, **www.ofsted.gov.uk**, or from the Ofsted publication order line: 0207 510 0180.

Again, whether or not you have received notice of inspection, it is well worth taking a look at Ofsted's *Handbooks for Inspecting Schools*:

Handbook for Inspecting Primary and Nursery Schools, TSO, 1999

Handbook for Inspecting Secondary Schools, TSO, 1999

Handbook for Inspecting Special Schools and Pupil Referral Units, TSO, 1999.

Stress Management

Anderson, B. (1999). *Meditation*. Piatkus, London.

Brennan, R. (2000). *Stress the Alternative Solution*. Foulsham, London.

Butler, D. (1999). *10-Minute Yoga*. Ward Lock, London.

Charles, R. (2000). *Your Mind's Eye*. Piatkus, London.

Peiffer, V. (1996). *Principles of Stress Management*. Thorsons, London.

Ryman, D. (1991). *Aromatherapy*. Piatkus, London.

Shapiro, D. and Shapiro, E. (1999). *Ultimate Relaxation*. Quadrille, London.

Wilson, P. (1997). *Calm at Work*. Penguin, London.

Wei Yue Sun, M.D. and Xiao Jing Li, M.D. (1999). *Tai Chi Ch'uan*. Sterling Publishing, New York.

Workplace Bullying

Adams, A. (1992). *Bullying at Work: How to Confront and Overcome it.* Virago.

Field, T. (1996). *Bully in Sight.* Success Unlimited.

Miscellaneous

Gardner, H. (1993). *Frames of Mind.* Fontana.

Goleman, D. (1996). *Emotional Intelligence.* Bloomsbury, London.

Goleman, D. (1998). *Working with Emotional Intelligence.* Bloomsbury, London.

Hare, B. (1988). *Be Assertive.* Vermilion, London.

Hindle, T. (1998). *Manage Your Time.* Dorling Kindersley, London.

Rechtschaffen, S. (1996). *Time Shifting.* Rider Books.

Useful addresses

Office for Standards in Education
Alexandra House
33 Kingsway
London
WC2 6SE

Telephone: 0207 421 6800
www.ofsted.gov.uk

OFSTED Publications Centre
PO Box 6927
London
E3 3NZ

Telephone: 0207 510 0180

Office for Standards in Inspection (OFSTIN)
9 Quatre Bras
Hexham
Northumberland
NE46 3JY

Telephone and fax: 01434 600134

Redress: The Bullied Teachers Support Network
Bramble House
Mason Drive
Hook
Near Goole
East Riding of Yorkshire
DN14 5NE

Telephone: 01405 764432

Organisations concerned with emotional literacy

**Antidote: Campaign for
Emotional Literacy**
5th Floor
45 Beech Street
London
EC2 8AD

Telephone: 020 7588 5151

E-mail: james@antidote.org.uk
www.antidote.org.uk

The Self-esteem Network
32 Carisbrooke Road
London
E17 7EF

Telephone: 020 8521 6977

E-mail:titus@gci.org.uk
(Membership joint with Antidote)

Re:membering Education
66 Beaconsfield Villas
Brighton
BN1 6HE

E-mail: remember@mcmail.com
www.remember.mcmail.com

Heartskills
35 Murray Road
Northwood
Middlesex
HA6 2YP

Telephone: 01923 820 900

E-mail: info@heartskillscoach.com
www.heartskillscoach.com

Index

Page numbers in **bold** refer to tables and boxes.

quality of curricular and other opportunities offered to pupils 37–43

quality of teaching 33–7

school's results and pupils' achievements 27–30

and standards 27–32

working with parents 46–8

evidence forms 16, 106

exclusions 30, 31, 32

exercise 177

expectations, high **148**

extra-curricular activities 37, 38, 43, 74

failure

dealing with **199**

requirement of special measures 193–200

fear(s) 167

examples of 140–7

organisational **141**

feedback 5, 6, 7, 11, 66, **75**, 77, 79–87, 92, 183–4

aims of inspectors 79

dealing with non-constructive 82–4

differences between written and oral **86**

disagreement over 82, 86

facing criticism 147–9

main barriers to hearing 80

observation of lessons by colleagues 107

and profile of teaching 84–5

purpose of **83**

reasons for feeling disgruntled about criticism 82

response to 80–1

short inspections 12, **85**

unfair criticism 146–7

utilising of 207–10

formal warning issuing of to schools 206–7

forms, pre-inspection 16, 56, **58**

'Fresh Start' school 198

From Failure to Success 198, 200

full inspection 10–11

ginger 177

Gingko Biloba 156

Ginseng 156

governors 49, 50, 51, 104, 186, **203–4**

grading

profile of judgement on quality of teaching 16–17, **24**, 84–5

receiving a lower than expected grade 146

Handbook for Inspecting Primary and Nursery Schools 30–1

Handbook for Inspecting Secondary Schools 31–2

Handbooks for Inspecting Schools 6, 22, 28–9, 34–5, 52, 59, **65, 71**, 81, 104, 107, 114, 183–4, 185

Hay McBer model, of teacher effectiveness 102–3

headteachers 174

relationship with inspectors 68

and run-up to inspection 52

health

tips for good 176–8

health and safety

of pupils 44, 45

health supplements
  using of in managing stress
    155–6, 177, 178
helpers
  relationship with inspectors 72–3
herbalism 173
HMCI (Her Majesty's Chief
  Inspector) 193, 195–6, 205
HMI (Her Majesty's Inspectors)
  1, 3, 11, 195–6, 197, 198, 205–6
hobbies 154, 173
homework 97
homeopathy 173
humour 179
hypnotherapy 173

ICT 50
immune system boosting
  supplements 178
improvements
  need for after inspection 53–4,
    187, 209
  need for if serious weaknesses
    are found 205–6
  setting your own targets for **191**
  since last inspection 26–7
induction 50
insomnia 175
Inspecting Schools: The Framework
  5, 8, **65**, 184–5
Inspection Notebook 17
inspection personnel 2–4
inspection report *see* report,
  inspection
inspection teams 57, 58
inspection window 2–3, 56
inspections *see* Ofsted inspections

inspectors 2–8, 57
  categories 3–4
  and Code of Conduct 5, 64, 66
  expected standards of 4–8, 66
  and giving feedback 81
  meetings with parents 2, 16, 47,
    56, 60–1
  need for base from which to work
    60
  obligations of 66
  pre-inspection preparations to be
    made by registered 63–4
  pre-inspection visit by registered
    59–60
  relationship and discussions with
    pupils 69–72, 135, **190**
  relationship and discussions with
    teachers 5, 6, 7, 66–9, 73,
    76–9, 81, 144
  relationship with other adults in
    classroom 72–3
  skills of 7

judgements 19, 183
  documents required to make
    62–3
  how they are made 15–17

Kava Kava 156

laughter 179
Lay Inspectors 3–4
leadership, quality of 24, 49–53
learning support 38
lesson plans 125
  effective **99**
  fear of not having enough time to
    complete 140–1

target setting **191**
Teacherline 169
   First Report (2000) 9
teachers
   and accountability 18–19
   caring for pupils 44–6
   effectiveness see effectiveness, teacher
   highlighting evidence of success 129–32
   inspection report in relation to 186
   knowing the extent of your job **112–13**
   managing paperwork 127–8
   meeting with registered inspector in pre-inspection visit 59–60
   positive aspects of inspection **74–5**
   preparation of pupils' work 126–7
   preparation of resources 125–6
   preparation of teaching/office space 132–4
   preparing pupils 134–6
   professional development portfolio **132**
   relationship and discussions with inspectors 5, 6, 7, 66–9, 73, 76–9, 81, 144
   relationship with parents 47, 48
   relationship with pupils 35, 36, 75, 100, 101, 135
   role in preparation 109–13
   and schemes of work 124–5, 145
   self-reflection focal points **129-31**
   unreasonable expectations of 141–2

teaching, quality of 33–7
teaching methods 33, 34–5, 36–7, 97
Team Inspectors 3, 4
tiredness 175, 177

under-inspection **71**
unions 91, 164, 200

visualisation techniques 173
vitamins 156

water 177
weaknesses
   in a school 205–6
Woodhead, Chris 69
work schemes see schemes of work
workload **14**, 160
Worthing High School 105

Zeal, Gareth 155